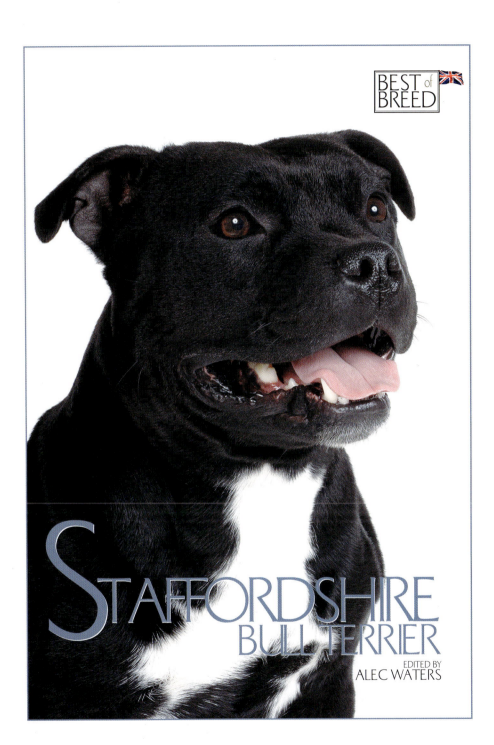

BEST of BREED

STAFFORDSHIRE BULL TERRIER

EDITED BY
ALEC WATERS

DEDICATION

This book is dedicated to Alec Waters.
Universally renowned and respected as judge, fearless competitor, and breeder of his world famous Ashstock
Staffordshire Bull Terriers, always willing to draw on his vast experience to unselfishly help others, a man to be
remembered for all the good he has done for the breed he loved so dearly.

ACKNOWLEDGEMENTS

The publishers would like to thank the following for help with photography: Sue Russell, Jeff Cockings,
Leanne Ferguson (Fergustaff), Jim Beaufoy (Wyrefare), Colin Davies (Mimcol), Alec Waters (Ashstock),
Jenny Smith (Willowstaff), Norma Vann (Vanoric), Terri Morrell, Jo-Ann Essex, Jan King, Marnie Wells, Jayne Winrow (Jayneze),
Alan Seymour, and Steve Hallifax for his excellent portraits of Staffordshire Bull Terriers.
Page 2 © istockphoto.com/Eline Spek; Page 63 © istockphoto.com/Jennifer Daley
Page 84 © istockphoto.com/Caziopeia

Special thanks to Archie Bryden (Gantocks) for his expert guidance on inherited disorders in Chapter 8.

Cover photo: © Tracy Morgan Animal Photography (www.animalphotographer.co.uk)

The British Breed Standard reproduced in Chapter 7 is the copyright of the Kennel Club and published with the club's kind
permission. Extracts from the American Breed Standard are reproduced by kind permission of the American Kennel Club.

THE QUESTION OF GENDER

The 'he' pronoun is used throughout this book in favour of the rather impersonal 'it', but no gender bias is intended.

First published in 2008 by The Pet Book Publishing Company Limited
PO Box 8 Lydney Gloucestershire GL15 6YD

This revised and updated edition first published in 2009
© 2009 Pet Book Publishing Company Limited.

ISBN
978-1-906305-19-2
1-906305-19-6

Printed and bound in Singapore.

CONTENTS

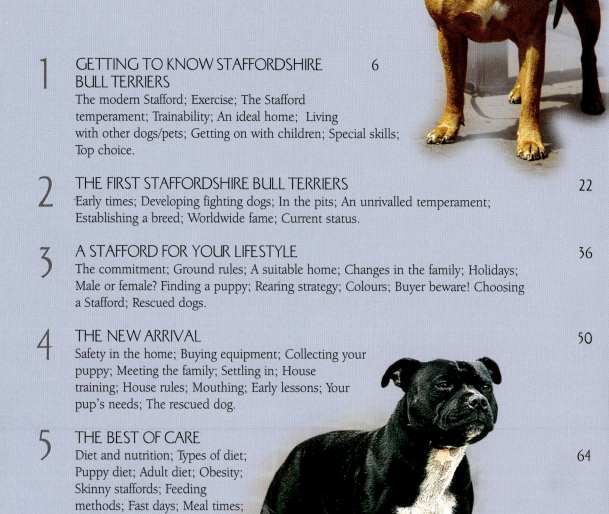

1 GETTING TO KNOW STAFFORDSHIRE   6
BULL TERRIERS
The modern Stafford; Exercise; The Stafford
temperament; Trainability; An ideal home; Living
with other dogs/pets; Getting on with children; Special skills;
Top choice.

2 THE FIRST STAFFORDSHIRE BULL TERRIERS   22
Early times; Developing fighting dogs; In the pits; An unrivalled temperament;
Establishing a breed; Worldwide fame; Current status.

3 A STAFFORD FOR YOUR LIFESTYLE   36
The commitment; Ground rules; A suitable home; Changes in the family; Holidays;
Male or female? Finding a puppy; Rearing strategy; Colours; Buyer beware! Choosing
a Stafford; Rescued dogs.

4 THE NEW ARRIVAL   50
Safety in the home; Buying equipment; Collecting your
puppy; Meeting the family; Settling in; House
training; House rules; Mouthing; Early lessons; Your
pup's needs; The rescued dog.

5 THE BEST OF CARE
Diet and nutrition; Types of diet;
Puppy diet; Adult diet; Obesity;   64
Skinny staffords; Feeding
methods; Fast days; Meal times;
Exercising your Stafford;
Grooming your Stafford;
Veterinary care; Saying
goodbye.

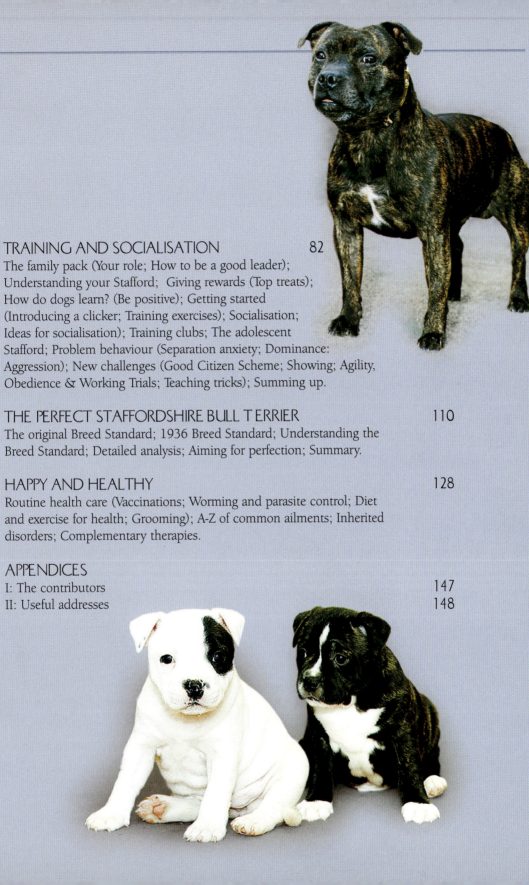

6 TRAINING AND SOCIALISATION   82

The family pack (Your role; How to be a good leader);
Understanding your Stafford; Giving rewards (Top treats);
How do dogs learn? (Be positive); Getting started
(Introducing a clicker; Training exercises); Socialisation;
Ideas for socialisation); Training clubs; The adolescent
Stafford; Problem behaviour (Separation anxiety; Dominance:
Aggression); New challenges (Good Citizen Scheme; Showing; Agility,
Obedience & Working Trials; Teaching tricks); Summing up.

7 THE PERFECT STAFFORDSHIRE BULL TERRIER   110

The original Breed Standard; 1936 Breed Standard; Understanding the
Breed Standard; Detailed analysis; Aiming for perfection; Summary.

8 HAPPY AND HEALTHY   128

Routine health care (Vaccinations; Worming and parasite control; Diet
and exercise for health; Grooming); A-Z of common ailments; Inherited
disorders; Complementary therapies.

APPENDICES

I: The contributors   147
II: Useful addresses   148

GETTING TO KNOW STAFFORDSHIRE BULL TERRIERS

Chapter 1

The Staffordshire Bull Terrier inherits its physical attributes and temperament from the bull and terrier crosses of the late 1700s and early 1800s, bred primarily for combat. The biting power, courage and tenacity of the Bulldog, coupled with the spirit and agility of the early terriers, created a sporting dog with renowned fighting ability. The Stafford's history has created a unique breed, as through his intimate relationship with his handler during life-threatening fights and afterwards when tending his injuries, a special bond between man and dog was forged. The physical size of the dog pits, and the need to manually handle and supervise the dogs during fights, meant that the dogs needed to be manageable and hence the Stafford is a relatively small dog, possessing great strength for its size.

THE MODERN STAFFORD

The Kennel Club Standard for the breed was originally drafted in 1935 and reflected the physical attributes of the early fighting dogs and is the blueprint for today's pet/show Stafford. Although now somewhat refined, the modern Stafford should be active, agile, and athletic, and, most importantly, should possess no exaggerations that might affect its health and welfare. The body should be muscular and well-defined with good width to chest, straight fronted and well-boned. The topline should be level with a degree of fall away at the croup, blending into a low-set 'pump handle' tail. The overall picture should be balanced, muscular and agile, and one that fits into an imaginary box.

SIZING UP

When viewed from above, there should be a good spring of rib and a defined waist. A Stafford should be 35.5 to 40.5 cm (14 to 16 in) high at the withers (the nape of the neck, or the point where the neck flows into the shoulders). Dogs should weigh 12.7 to 17 kg (28 to 38 lb), and bitches should weigh 11 to 15.4 kg (24 to 34 lb). These weights should be in proportion to the height, and should convey balance and strength without coarseness or excessive 'bulliness'. Although the aforementioned heights/weights are quoted in the Kennel Club Breed Standard (also adopted by the American Kennel Club Standard), it has to be said that today's modern show dog errs towards the top end of these limits.

HEAD BREED

The head should be wedge-shaped with a broad skull, discernible stop and a strong,

The Staffordshire Bull Terrier is an active, athletic dog with a balanced, muscular build.

broad muzzle of medium length. On no account should the muzzle be over-short, which could lead to breathing problems. Ideally, the length of the muzzle should be approximately one third of the total length from the tip of the nose to the occiput (i.e. back of the skull). Although a prominent feature of the Stafford, the head should not be extreme and should remain in balance with the body and free from excess flesh, particularly around the muzzle and flews (lips). Breeding for exaggeration of any

kind is to be avoided, as this often leads to unnecessary whelping difficulties.

The eyes should be set to look straight ahead; they should be set wide apart, round and of medium size. The colour of the eyes can bear some resemblance to the coat colour, but should preferably be dark to enhance the desired expression; the eye rims should also be dark. More importantly, the eyes should not be over-large and protruding, which would have been a great disadvantage to a fighting dog.

A Stafford's ears can be half pricked, but a rose ear is better and gives a softer, more typical expression. Ears should be low set and, ideally, not over-large or heavy; full drop or pricked ears are not typical and are highly undesirable.

Teeth should be large and regular and form a scissor bite (i.e. where the top incisors closely overlap the bottom incisors). All four points of the canines should be visible with the jaw tightly shut. Minor dentition problems can be tolerated, but badly overshot and undershot mouths are to be avoided, and bottom canines that dig into the roof of the mouth (referred to as 'inverted' or 'converging' canines), are highly undesirable. The 'overshot' mouth is where the top incisors extend well past the lower incisors, creating a definite gap. However, it should be borne in mind that the younger puppy can often appear overshot while his head and jaw are developing. This is perfectly normal and by maturity he will usually have a correct scissor bite. The dog with an 'undershot' mouth is often referred to as a 'grinner', and, as one might expect, this is where the upper teeth fit inside the lower teeth, reminiscent of the Bulldog, and is a throwback to that early breeding.

COAT AND COLOURS

The Stafford should have a short, tight-fitting coat and this should be smooth-textured. Standard colours are red, fawn, white, black or blue, or any one of these colours with white. Any shade of brindle, or any shade of brindle with white, is also acceptable. Although highly undesirable, black and tan and liver are both recognised colours and will occasionally appear in litters. These are associated with 'throwbacks' to the historical use of Manchester Terriers in the early crosses, or may sometimes occur when breeders have experimented with colours.

Liver puppies exhibit a brownish/golden coat colour at birth, but, as they get older, this becomes a more grey/brown or reddish colour, frequently with light nails, yellow or blue eyes, and a reddish nose (often referred to as a 'Dudley' nose).

The black and tan Staffords are not to be confused with a 'mismarked brindle', which is a brindle with random areas of red (or tan as it is sometimes called). For a Stafford to be classed as

The head is wedge-shaped, with dark eyes set to look straight ahead.

STAFFORD COLOURS
Acceptable colours

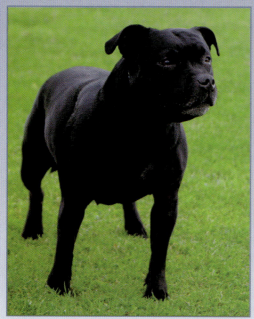

Black.

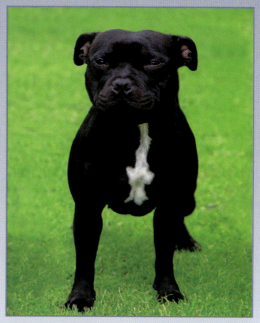

Black and white.

Red.

Red and white.

Acceptable colours

Brindle.

Pied – white and black

White with black markings.

White with fawn patches.

Blue and white.

Undesirable colours

Liver with white markings. Note the 'Dudley' nose.

This puppy has black and tan markings, and, unusually, a white patch on the neck and chest.

black and tan, only two colours are present, and the tan must be prominent (i.e. there must be definite swathes of tan) on the feet, legs, muzzle and chest. These markings are akin to those exhibited by such breeds as the Rottweiler, Dobermann and Manchester Terrier. As previously advised, neither of these colours is desirable and would be heavily penalised in the show ring.

Another colour that seems to be extremely 'fashionable' is the blue Stafford and variances of blue with white. Although these colours are within the Breed Standard, they are not popular in the show ring, and so most breeders do not actively try to reproduce these

colours. In essence a blue is a diluted black/brindle and often has light nails and eyes. I have rarely, if ever, seen a 'good one', and, indeed, I cannot think of any that regularly appear on the show circuit at this present time.

Unfortunately, there are 'hobby breeders' who seem to be actively seeking to reproduce these colours purely for profit, and they are duping the unsuspecting public into paying inflated sums of money for these so-called 'rare' Staffords. I would stress that if you particularly want a blue, then you should not expect to pay any more than the average asking price for a Kennel Club registered, health-checked Stafford.

EXERCISE
Although Staffords will accept varying levels of exercise according to the owner's availability and preference, there is no doubt that a dog with such high intelligence needs to be occupied. The more time you devote to your Stafford, the happier he will be, and, on balance, the less troublesome he will be.

GROWING PUPPIES
A young puppy should not be subjected to any rigorous exercise, and although it is a temptation for the proud owner to show off their new charge as soon as the veterinary surgeon gives the 'all clear' following inoculations, this

Staffords are individuals, and you should tailor exercise to suit your dog's needs.

should not be excessive. Prior to six months of age he will only require moderate exercise with free running and light lead work over short periods of time, and no intensive roadwork. During this time a puppy's bones are soft and 'too much too young' can result in malformed limbs and arthritis in later life. A puppy's exercise should be gradually increased so that by around 12 months he will be able to accompany his owner on long walks without distress.

TAILORING NEEDS

The Stafford benefits from regular exercise and responds well to training, all of which should be of an appropriate duration, dependent on age. Apart from the obvious health advantages to both dog and owner, a daily exercise routine assists in reducing the possibility of your dog seeking other diversions, such as chewing or causing mischief. You must always be

aware that, like humans, dogs vary in their make, shape and capabilities. Even at maturity not all dogs can withstand very long walks, and you need to tailor the exercise regime to that which is reasonable for your dog. A dog cannot speak for himself, so you have to be sensitive to his needs and also bear in mind the weather conditions and terrain. Always ensure you carry a supply of drinking water when embarking on a longer walk.

Staffords, like any other dogs, enjoy chasing and retrieving balls and similar objects – however, some of these games can become obsessive. Repetitive throwing of a ball over short distances, over hard standing and/or rough terrain can put undue pressure on the shoulder and knee joints and result in joint or ligament damage that can be crippling in later life, so bear this in mind and think for your dog. Ensure the ball (which should be of

sufficient size so there is no possibility of swallowing) bounces high enough for him to retrieve mid-air and preferably perform this exercise on a reasonably soft surface.

THE OLDER STAFFORD

It would be remiss of me not to include a few words about the 'oldies', for they enjoy and benefit from exercise too. The older dog who no longer has either the confidence or speed to walk with his younger kennelmates should not be confused with one not wishing to walk at all. Providing there is no physical impediment, oldies can be taken out individually at their own pace and allowed to meander a little; yes, it does take slightly longer, but it is important to have patience and consideration. A contented dog will live a longer, healthier life, and, after years of loyalty, that's the very least they deserve.

The Stafford stands out as being remarkably good with children.

THE STAFFORD TEMPERAMENT

"Bold, fearless and totally reliable." This is the description of the Staffordshire Bull Terrier's temperament in the Breed Standard. It is the unique history of the Stafford that makes him such a special dog. Originally bred as a fighting dog and famed for his ferocity in the pit, the Stafford also proved to be an excellent companion and was very good with children. In fact, it was not unknown for an injured dog to be transported home in a pram with the baby!

Around the 1800s the pit dogs (as they were then known) were a favourite with the poorest of families who not only fought them, but also worked them against badgers or as ratters to provide valuable extra income and so called 'entertainment'. The Stafford was therefore an exceptional dog of the time – a sort of 'Jekyll and Hyde'; on the one hand he had to be an excellent working dog, but on the other hand he had to be totally reliable and have affinity with humans and children, living as he did in the family home.

It is this historical special relationship with humans that makes the Staffordshire Bull Terrier the foremost family dog he is today, often warmly referred to as the 'Nanny Dog'. He is affectionate and tactile and more comfortable sharing your home or indeed your lap than spending long periods of time on his own in a kennel. Of course, if you do not relish this kind of close interaction with your dog, then you should consider whether a Stafford is actually the correct breed of dog for you. It should be borne in mind that the cute little puppy you first bring home will mature into a powerful and muscular animal, and the males, particularly, require a strong arm to control the lead. Staffords love human contact and will often be boisterous with visitors – you have to be prepared for the fact that not all your friends will appreciate this. Because of his close relationship with humans, the Stafford does not make a good guard dog and is not suited to being left for long periods without outside stimulation.

RESPONSIBLE OWNERSHIP

The Stafford has a colourful history. Do not forget that, while he loves people, he will react if challenged by another dog. For this reason you must always be a responsible owner and never take your dog into a public place unless he is on a collar and lead. Staffords do respond well to training, and it is a good idea to socialise your dog as widely as possible and as early as possible. However, although a Stafford may tolerate some dogs, he is unlikely to react kindly to a challenge, so always be vigilant and never leave your dog unattended.

It is recommended that where there are two or more Staffords in a household, they should be separated if left unattended.

Staffords sometimes 'mouth' (lightly clasp your wrist/forearm in their mouths), or tug at your sleeves. There is nothing sinister in this, but it can be a little disconcerting, particularly to visitors; therefore these practices are to be discouraged with a firm 'no'. It is a much simpler task to instil discipline and good manners in a young puppy than try to correct bad habits in the older dog.

The Stafford is well suited to a close-living relationship with his human companions – he is highly intelligent and thrives on a one-to-one basis, being ever eager to please, and he will give you a lifetime of devotion.

Staffordshire Bull Terriers that live together can be great friends and will play together, but it is advisable to separate them at times when they cannot be supervised.

TRAINABILITY

Early socialisation is very important in order to teach an acceptable interaction with other dogs, and this, coupled with basic obedience skills, is the way forward for our breed in today's dog-intolerant society. Remember that your actions reflect on the breed as a whole – a trained dog is a happy and socially acceptable dog. Most veterinary surgeries hold socialisation classes for puppies between eight and 14 weeks of age. At such classes your Stafford puppy will meet several breeds of dog at a very early age, and this may help to make him more tolerant. Following vaccinations, your dog can move on to the puppy classes, which include basic obedience and socialisation skills, thus paving the way for any form of training you may wish to pursue.

Because he is a highly intelligent animal, the Stafford responds exceptionally well to one-to-one training. As with any breed of dog, successful training depends on patience, repetition and reward. A Stafford is extremely eager to please and it is usually just a case of channelling this exuberant energy in the right direction – then there should be no limit to what you can achieve. (For more information on training, see Chapter Six.)

AN IDEAL HOME

A Stafford will adapt to his surroundings, and providing he has the required human contact and is given time, attention and exercise, he will thrive in most environments. The critical thing with a Stafford is to ensure that he has sufficient stimulation. He is highly intelligent and does not flourish if left for long periods unattended or without human contact. Therefore, if you want a kennel dog or a guard dog, this is definitely not the correct breed of dog for you.

Keeping a Stafford in a flat is not recommended unless someone is there most of the time, and that person needs to be active and able to take the dog out regularly. As with any breed of dog, a rural home probably offers the ideal environment, with the lack of heavy traffic and endless walks on the doorstep. However, not everyone can or indeed wishes to live in the country, and I know of many people who live in built-up areas and their Staffords are just as happy. The key factor is human companionship: a Stafford will live happily anywhere, provided he receives this in abundance together with a reasonable level of exercise and stimulation.

Wherever you live, a Stafford should ideally have access to a garden, which must be secure and fully dog-proof, and this should be completed prior to purchasing your puppy. Staffords are tenacious and will find the slightest hole, particularly if the neighbour's cat or pet dog insists

This is a breed that thrives on human companionship.

on 'teasing' them from the other side of the fence! Therefore, you should be observant and repair any damage as soon as it occurs. Because of his friendly disposition, a Stafford can easily fall victim to 'dog nappers'; for this reason you must ensure your garden is secure and that you can observe your dog at all times. Indeed, if security is in any doubt, then don't leave him unattended in your garden. Staffords are fearless and often become the victims of road traffic accidents. For this reason always ensure your dog is unable to rush out of a door or gate directly on to a road.

LIVING WITH OTHER DOGS/PETS

If correctly introduced, there is no reason why a Stafford should not live harmoniously with other dogs or pets within the home. If the Stafford is the 'new boy' then allow him to get used to his surroundings on first arriving at the home, then gradually introduce the other pets while keeping vigilant for any disagreements. Don't allow a puppy too much leeway with an older dog, as their milk teeth are like razors and can cause distress. However, it has to be said that dogs usually have their own way of putting 'junior' in his place if he oversteps the mark!

It is important when introducing a new puppy not to forget the older/existing pets that may, or may not, be Staffords. It is a little akin to bringing home a new baby – be sure to introduce

The male Stafford will aspire to be top dog if bitches are kept in the home.

the baby slowly but include the others. Be careful not to make the other dogs jealous, and, hopefully, you will ease the new arrival into the pack and all should live harmoniously. However, nothing can be guaranteed and it pays to remain watchful of the situation.

Away from the home, it is a good idea to teach your puppy to have respect for all sorts of animals, ranging from meeting horses and other dogs to farm animals that may be encountered on walks. The more animals and breeds of dog a Stafford encounters, the less fazed he will be. In the past, we have successfully kept a cat with seven Staffords, although she walked very slowly in their company!

Staffords will also live harmoniously in a pack, but it is not wise to have two Stafford dogs together when there are also bitches in the home. As the males mature, they will challenge for the 'top dog' status, and, if a bitch has seasons, this will further exacerbate the situation. Staffords should not be left unattended in numbers, as something as trivial as a knock at the door can be enough to trigger excitement, which can quickly turn into a fight; if you are not around to referee, then the outcome can be unpleasant.

Crates can be a useful feature when separating animals when the owner is away from the home for short periods. However, Staffords are not meant to be cooped up in crates for long periods of time, so if you use a crate, please don't abuse it. You have to be careful of rough games between Staffords, or indeed any other breed of dog that you may own, as these can sometimes flare up and become out of control. If dogs have a tendency to quarrel, then they are best left in different rooms while you are away from the home.

GETTING ON WITH CHILDREN

The Stafford is the fifth most popular breed of dog in the UK, and one of the very few where there is a specific reference in the Kennel Club Breed Standard to his affinity with people and children. He is "highly intelligent and affectionate, especially with children". The Stafford is indeed a complex dog, and some people have difficulty understanding how he can be involved in a heated exchange with another dog one minute, yet moments later gently accept a treat from the fingers of a small child. However, no matter how reliable the breed, it is always advisable to exercise caution where children and animals are concerned, and they should never be left alone without parental supervision.

Children need to be taught that a dog is a living animal with feelings and not a toy, and both child and dog should be taught to respect each other. Teach your dog to accept treats by hand, to wait patiently and accept the food gently, and don't allow him to 'snap' at food. Don't permit your child to wake your Stafford when he is sleeping or constantly handle him when he is awake. Always ensure a puppy has his own sleeping area where he can retire when he is tired, or where you can place him if he or the child is having one of those exuberant moments. Teach your child that the puppy's bed is where he is to be left undisturbed. If necessary, separate them by using a child gate or playpen. Alternatively, a folding crate can be useful and convenient for short periods of time.

A puppy's milk teeth are extremely sharp and he should be discouraged from biting, as it can be very painful, particularly for a child. Encourage children to sit when handling young puppies, as this minimises the

A Stafford will strike up a close bond with a child, but a situation of mutual respect must be established.

risk of accidents. Don't allow your child to be spiteful and smack the puppy. A puppy should know his place in the pack and respect the child, but he only needs to be firmly told 'no' when he is doing wrong and he will quickly learn. His main training should come from the adults in the household who can exercise consistency, otherwise he will be confused. Don't foster jealousy or rough play or taunt the dog, as this sends out the wrong messages and encourages aggressive interaction between the dog and people.

Never leave a child solely in charge of a Stafford on a walk. When a Stafford is taken for a walk, or is anywhere outside the confines of the home, children and youngsters should be accompanied by an adult (preferably the owner). There is a risk that they can be targeted by dog thieves, who could easily snatch a dog from a child. Another concern is that the adult Stafford is a powerful animal and this, coupled with their dislike of other dogs, means that adult supervision is required on walks. Much of the aforementioned is commonsense, and, with a few basic rules observed, dog and child will grow up together as the best of friends, and each will contribute to making a fuller life for the other.

As mentioned earlier, the Stafford is affectionately known as the 'Nanny Dog' due to his special relationship with children. I have known Staffords skateboard, swim and play

A Stafford can form a truly special bond with his owners, and none more so than an assistance dog. Here Gillian McCluskey is pictured with her seizure alert dog Harvey, trained by UK charity Support Dogs.

football with children, and even play hide-and-seek with them – actually running to hide and waiting for the children to find him! Living with and looking after a Stafford is an excellent way of teaching a child respect for animals and responsibility for their well-being, and in return they will have a friend for life.

SPECIAL SKILLS

As we have seen, the Staffordshire Bull Terrier is intelligent and highly trainable, and he has the ability to form a close bond with his owner. This is highlighted in the case of Gillian McCluskey

and her Support Dog, Harvey, who is specially trained to alert Gillian when she is about to have a seizure. This gives her the opportunity to get to a safe place, or to take medication before the onset of the seizure. Gillian tells her story:

"I have had epilepsy for 36 years, and the medical profession has been unsuccessful in finding a method of controlling my seizures. Nine years ago I was told that I had another medical condition which increased the frequency of my attacks.

Saffy brings a special kind of Stafford magic into people's lives

"I heard about the work of the Support Dogs charity, and after completing my applications and assessments, I was told that I might be a suitable candidate. Soon afterwards, Support Dogs telephoned me to say they had a small black Staffordshire Bull Terrier named Harvey, and would I be interested? I could hardly believe it!

"Harvey and I bonded straight away – I knew we were meant for each other. We underwent a total of six weeks' intensive training and eight months later Harvey qualified

as a seizure alert dog.

"Since then, having Harvey as an 'early warning system' has almost reduced my seizure frequency to nil, except when my other medical condition flares up. I have also regained my self confidence and live a much better quality of life. Harvey knows before I am going to have a seizure and he looks after me. My doctor is now reducing my medication because she believes Harvey is my remedy.

"Where I go, Harvey goes! I can't imagine what life would be like without him. He's my

best friend and my life has taken on a new meaning with him by my side."

THERAPY DOGS

The Staffordshire Bull Terrier has also proved to be an excellent therapy dog, as his affectionate nature makes him ideal in this role.

In the UK, the charity for therapy dogs is known as PAT Dogs (Pets as Therapy). At present Pets As Therapy have 33 Staffordshire Bull Terriers working throughout the UK out of a total 3,000 dogs and 92 cats.

These PAT dogs and cats all provide a wonderful service to patients of all ages and disabilities in the community, visiting hospitals, hospices, residential homes, day care centres, special needs schools and many other establishments.

Most Staffords make excellent PAT dogs due to their intrinsic love of people, and, of course, temperament is of paramount importance – all dogs have to be 'bomb-proof'. The Stafford's intolerance of other dogs is not a burning issue, as there is only ever one PAT dog visiting at any one time. The stumbling block with Staffords, as one might imagine, is their joie de vivre! For obvious reasons they cannot be allowed to be boisterous in the vicinity of the old and infirm, and this tendency will mean that some are unsuitable.

Terri Morrell has two PAT dogs: Saffy (Subaron Sapphire Senorita) and Ralfie (Niatona the Boy Wonder) both of whom have also had successful show careers. Saffy gained RCC at Crufts a few years ago and Ralphie was placed second in his class in 2007. On both occasions, the rosettes were taken to show the patients and all were delighted at their success.

Saffy is now eight years old but still loves her visits – she was a natural when it came to training, whereas new recruit Ralphie has a completely different temperament and was somewhat more challenging. However, the key to success with even the more stubborn ones appears to be early training and socialisation with other dogs, but even this will not necessarily guarantee PAT dog success. Ralphie was PAT assessed at Crufts 2006. The situations he encountered and had to remain totally unfazed by were such things as walking through crowds, sudden noises and being approached by people in wheelchairs, with walking sticks and wearing baseball caps. He also had to demonstrate he could be picked up (in case of an emergency when visiting an establishment) – of course, this didn't worry him at all! Needless to say, he passed with flying colours.

TOP CHOICE

There are many positive virtues to owning a Stafford – he is a dog with special qualities that makes him an ideal family dog that is good with children. They are of medium size and their short coats are easy to keep clean and groom. Kept fit and active you can expect a normal, healthy

Stafford to live for an average 10-12 years. However, they can live for much longer and we ourselves are fortunate to have kept a dog until he was over 17 and several others who were between 14-16 years when they died. Most Staffords are hardy animals and provided they are regularly exercised and have a good-quality diet, they suffer few ailments.

I hope the foregoing paragraphs have given you an insight into the versatility of this wonderful breed of dog. There really is a wealth of activities you can pursue with him, or you can enjoy him simply as a companion. Congratulations on selecting this wonderful breed of dog. I am sure you will find in him a true companion and life-long friend, you will have lots of fun together and your life will undoubtedly never be quite the same again. Remember: you're never alone if you own a Stafford!

Once you have chosen a Stafford, you will never want to be without one.

THE FIRST STAFFORDSHIRE BULL TERRIERS

Chapter 2

There he stands, alert and ready for anything the day has to offer him. A subtle blend of Bull and Terrier, a middleweight of a dog rather than a heavyweight and with an honest expression in his eyes, which, together with his strong and muscular frame, so readily reveals the very history of his breed. A veritable symbol depicting his origins long ago from the Black Country area of Britain, here is a dog that today is firmly established throughout the world in the homes of those who cherish him for his courage, loyalty and affection to his family. This is the Staffordshire Bull Terrier, a fabulous pet and show dog with a fascinating, colourful, yet often cruel history that depicts the rise from the most humble of beginnings to the heights of one of the world's leading breeds. Here is a dog whose loyal temperament and character have always shone through to survive whatever hard times have befallen him.

EARLY TIMES

Long before the commencement of the Christian era, the Phoenicians plied the shores of Britain for trade. From these very early times, it is believed that the origins of what is known today as the Staffordshire Bull Terrier first arrived. The traders brought dogs with them, which were readily accepted by the Ancient Britons. These large, fighting dogs of the Mastiff type were domesticated and trained by the early Britons to fight, and this they did with

Dogs of war, of the Mastiff type, were used in combat against the first Roman invaders of Britain.

Bear-baiting: An engraving by Harry Alken, London c 1820.

great courage and ferocity. They were successfully used in combat against the first Roman invaders of Britain. The Romans were so impressed by these dogs and their gladiatorial capabilities that they shipped many of them back to Rome to show their fighting capabilities when pitted in the arenas there in various 'sports' of the times.

The influence of these earliest Mastiffs quickly spread outwards from Rome throughout large areas of Europe, with much influence in the formative breeding of a number of breeds in that continent. These early Mastiffs were described as long ago as AD8 by Gratius Faliscus as the "Pugnaces of Britain" and as the "broad mouthed dogs" of Britain by the poet Claudian. These 'Pugnaces' or Mastiffs are regarded as among the early

ancestors of the Bulldog. Much later from that source, over a period of many centuries, the Staffordshire Bull Terrier became firmly established in Britain without any marked variation in stature or type.

Shortly after the Norman conquest of Britain, it was recorded that these dogs were being used for bull, bear and lion baiting in the now growing sporting activities of that era. Around the year 1400, writers were describing a fearsome dog of great strength, size and courage, large and heavy of head and with a short muzzle. The dog was called the "Alaunt", which was used for hunting large game. The description of this type of dog shows that it appeared to be directly descended from the 'Pugnaces', and from this dog, certain

varieties of the Bulldog developed.

Later, in the 16th and early part of the 17th century, other names associated with this dog started to appear, such as 'Bull-dogge', the 'Mastyve' and the 'Mastie'. These can be associated with the heightening in fashion of the sport of bull baiting, from the middle of the 16th to the middle of the 17th centuries. This sport appears to have originated in about the year 1209, some 200 years after bear baiting. Both bull and bear baiting had the approval status of Royal patronage, and had become very fashionable among the higher reaches of society. Cities and towns around Britain had their 'bull rings', and these named sites are still in evidence today, long after the so-called 'sports' had been banned by law.

The popularity of these sporting activities was immense. Throughout Britain they flourished with tremendous spectator support at bear gardens, bull rings, and at fairs and wakes. The sport of bull baiting, the origin of the very existence of the breed of dogs that eventually became the Staffordshire Bull Terrier, was more popular with spectators than bear baiting. This was due to the comparative slowness of the sport and subsequent loss of gate money. Now, however, bull baiting was also deemed to be in decline. Both bull and bear baiting, which had been under Royal patronage, had almost disappeared by 1750, to be finally made illegal in 1835.

DEVELOPING FIGHTING DOGS

The original dogs used to fight in the pits were very much the same dogs that were used for baiting the bulls. The Bulldogs of the time, though brave, ferocious and fearless animals and ideal for 'pinning a bull', did not satisfactorily provide what the sporting gentlemen of the period required. Bulldogs had proved to be slow, heavy and cumbersome in a one-to-one dog fight, and so the breeders of fighting dogs turned their attention to something smaller and lighter. They required a dog with the undoubted fierceness, tenacity and courage of the then Bulldog, with the speed, agility and athleticism of a smaller and lighter dog.

There are two differing theories advocated as to the exact patterns of breeding that took place to produce the ideal dog fighter, which would eventually become named the Staffordshire Bull Terrier some 130 to 140 years later. Either, or perhaps both, theories may possibly be true.

The first theory is that the original Bulldog that existed around 1800 was not generally crossed with any other smaller breed at all. To become the true

DOG AGAINST DOG

Following the decline of bull and bear baiting, the sporting gentlemen's attention now turned to another dubious sport: organised dog fighting, which can be traced back to around, or just before, the commencement of the 18th century. For a period of about 100 years organised dog fighting had taken place, but somewhat in the shadow of the still popular sports of bull and bear baiting. This change of emphasis was to turn out to be a further step in the development of what was to become the Staffordshire Bull Terrier – but much was to come about before this, accompanied by a great deal of suffering and cruelty to many wonderful dogs. So now, around the year 1800 and at the time of comparative decline in bull baiting, it was the turn of the poorer sections of the community to take on the mantle of so-called organised 'sport'. This was dog fighting, where man pitted dog against dog for gain, and which was always at the dog's expense.

fighting 'pit dog' he was selectively bred along smaller, lighter and more terrier-like lines, with very little or no impact from any direct terrier breeding. The 'lay-back' in the muzzle of the Bulldog would have been selectively bred out, a task not considered beyond the capabilities of experienced breeders of the times.

A study of the famous Abraham Cooper 1816 painting of typical Bulldogs of the period gives some credibility to this theory, as do those of other artists of the time. His depiction in his painting of 'Crib' and 'Rosa' are considered

representations of the finest-bred Bulldogs of the day. The dogs show in the quarters, bodies and whip tails, a conformation very much more along terrier lines than anything suggested by the modern Bulldog of today, and certainly similar to the conformation of the Staffordshire Bull Terrier as we know it. Clearly the modern Staffordshire Bull Terrier more closely resembles the conformation of his direct ancestors than the modern Bulldog and his ancestors. This theory is certainly a fascinating one and especially so with the suggestion that the Staffordshire Bull Terrier emerged along pure and virtually unadulterated bloodlines directly from the Bulldog of old.

The second theory is that the original Bulldog, weighing in at about 60 lb or 27 kg, was crossed with a smaller and lighter terrier weighing about 20 lb of 9 kg. This was to produce an ideal fighting dog with all the strength, stamina, ferocity and courage of the original Bulldog, and the speed, agility, activity and athleticism of the terrier. The now extinct Old English Terrier is the dog considered the most likely terrier to have been used for the purpose. This was a terrier similar in build and

Crib and Rosa: Detail from an engraving after a painting by Abraham Cooper.

Bull and Terrier – oil painting c 1830.

conformation to the modern day Manchester Terrier, and would certainly have fulfilled the requirements. However, if this theory is to be accepted, then it is also likely that many experiments were carried out with the breeding of the dogs to fight in the pits. The breeders of the day certainly were not interested in what the dogs looked like, but only in the ability of a dog that would win fights when pitted for money against other dogs. One thing is clear, however: whatever cross-breeding took place, it involved the original Bulldog and a faster and lighter terrier, to produce the dog to best fight in the pit.

More than likely, the prominent breeders used their most successful fighting dogs as both sires and dams in any

breeding programmes, and it was the emphasis on fighting ability that was the required essential feature in their selections. The matings of the original Bulldogs with any terrier type of dog or bitch of the day that displayed gameness and agile tenacity is a distinct possibility, when taking into consideration the end requirements. The theory of the matings of Bulldog to terrier to produce the desired fighting dog of the 'pit' is backed up by the writings of the 19th century authors with their references to the terms 'Bull Terrier', 'Bulldog-Terrier' and 'Bull-and-Terrier'.

IN THE PITS

In acceptance that the former theory of selective Bulldog breeding has credibility, the

general belief is that the 'Bull and Terrier' of the 19th century emerged from the crossing of the original Bulldog and a terrier, which was more than likely to have been the Old English Terrier from about 1800 onwards, although perhaps even earlier than that. Whatever the explanation, here was a fighting dog of tremendous strength, agility and skill, seemingly impervious to pain, with a tremendous ability to both give and receive punishment in the pit. Not to be forgotten is a vitally important factor that has proved to be a major contribution towards his survival as a breed. That was, and is today, an unrivalled soundness plus reliability of temperament towards his masters, who in so many instances in those early

Wasp, Child and Billy: Detail from a hand-coloured engraving after a painting by H.B. Chalon, 1809. These dogs were from a fighting kennel owned by the Duke of Hamilton.

days did not deserve it.

From the period commencing in about 1790, serious attention was given to matching dog against dog, rather than dog against bull or bear. The fighting of dogs had been organised for well over a 100 years before that time, but had been overshadowed by the more prominent sports of bull and bear baiting. Now, with the decline in popularity of the tormenting of bull and bear, the arrival on the so-called sporting scene of the lighter and more agile 'Bull and Terrier' was to completely change the emphasis to that of the organised dog fight.

During the early 19th century, dog pits were to be found everywhere. Often patronised by the aristocracy, organised dog fights abounded. Dog was pitted against dog, weight for weight, in fights strictly controlled by rules. Gameness was the key, and great sums of money were betted and paid for the winning dogs. After 1835 when the baiting and fighting sports had been made illegal, the dog fights carried on. In spite of any laws, it was most difficult to track down and stop the organised dog fight, which, by the will and determination of the organisers, successfully managed to keep one step ahead of the police. To the vast majority of reasonable people, the sickening sight of a dog maiming and sometimes killing another dog would have been absolutely horrifying. Not so to those who championed the sport. To these people it was fair combative conflict between two animals that were trained to fight, wanted to fight, were fearless and fought 'fairly' pound for pound under strict rules. Sadly, the grim reality was that these noble dogs were controlled by ruthless and uncaring masters.

Despite the attention of the police and legal authorities, the determination of the proprietors and organisers of dog fighting can well be imagined by taking a look at an example of a form of agreement drawn up in preparation of an organised dog fight. Perhaps attention should be drawn to the cold-blooded, clinical ruthlessness addressed to the plight and welfare of the dogs, and the 'portability' of the fighting scene in the event of pending police involvement. All this was for the satisfaction of blood lust and gambling, with the dog as the possible sacrifice.

ARTICLES OF AGREEMENT

Articles of Agreement made on the....................day of....................18....................
....agrees to fight his....................dog................pounds weight against....................
dog.........pounds weight, for £...........a side at...
on the........day of..............18.....

The dogs to be weighed at....................o'clock in the....................and fight between....................o'clock and
o'clock in the ....

The deposits to be made as in hereafter mentioned; to be delivered to...
(who is to be the final Stakeholder), namely, the first deposit of £....................a side

at the making of the match; the second deposit of £....................a side

on the....................of....................at the house of.......................................; third deposit of £................

on the....................of....................at the house of.......................................; fourth deposit of £..............

on the....................of....................at the house of.......................................; fifth deposit of £................

on the....................of....................at the house of.......................................; ....;

which is the last.

Rules

1st   To be a fair fight....................yards from scratch.

2nd   Both dogs to be tasted before and after fighting if required.

3rd   Both dogs to be shewn fair to the scratch, and washed at their own corners.

4th   Both seconds to deliver the dogs fair from the corner, and not leave until the dogs commence fighting.

5th   A Referee to be chosen in the pit; one minute time to be allowed between every fair go away; fifty seconds
allowed for sponging; and at the expiration of that time the timekeeper shall call make ready, and as soon as
the minute is expired the dogs to be delivered, and the dog refusing or stopping on the way to be the loser.

6th   Should either second pick up his dog in a mistake, he shall put it down. Immediately, by order of the Referee,
or the money to be forfeited.

7th   Should anything precarious be found on either dog, before or after fighting in the pit, the backers of the dog
so found to forfeit, and the person holding the battle money, to give it up immediately when called upon to
do so.

Alas, little of comfort or support in the above for the welfare of the courageous and brave dogs that were so often severely maimed and even lost their lives for the monetary gain of their owners when they won, and with contempt and often cruelty when they lost. Incredible though it was, here was a dog who would willingly fight to the death to please his owner. After being outlawed in 1835, the fighting of dogs continued, but it now became a strictly underground activity with an ever-increasing loss in general acceptability in the eyes of the public.

AN UNRIVALLED TEMPERAMENT

Perhaps more than anything else, it was the unique temperament, love and trust of people that ensured the survival of this dog from most humble beginnings. After all, here was a dog, later to be named the Staffordshire Bull

8th   Referee to be chosen in the pit before fighting, whose decision in all cases shall be final.

9th   Either dog exceeding the stipulated weight on the day of the weighing to forfeit the money deposited.

10th In the case of a dog being declared dead by the Referee, the living dog shall remain at him for ten minutes when he shall be taken to his corner if it be his turn to scratch, or if it be the dead dog's turn the fight shall be at end by order of the Referee.

11th In the case of Police interference the Referee to name the next place and time of fighting, on the same day if possible, and day by day until it be decided, but if no Referee be chosen, the Stakeholder to name the next place and time; but if a Referee has been chosen and then refuses to name the next place and time of fighting, or goes away after being disturbed, then the power of choosing the next time and place be left with the Stakeholder and a fresh Referee be chosen in the pit and the power of the former one be entirely gone.

12th In case of Police interference and the dogs have commenced fighting they will not be required to weigh any more; but if they have not commenced fighting they will have to weigh day by day at......lb. until decided at the time and place named by the Referee, or if he refuses and goes away, then the Stakeholder has to name the time and place.

13th The seconder of either dog is upon no consideration to call his adversary's dog by name while in the pit, nor use anything whatever in his hands with which to call off his dog.

14th To toss up the night before fighting for the place of fighting, between the hours of ....and.......o'clock at the house where the last deposit is made.

15th The above stakes are not to be given up until fairly won or lost by a fight, unless either party break the above agreement.

16th All deposits to be made between the hours of.......... and.........o'clock at night.

17th Either party not following up or breaking the above agreement, to forfeit the money down.

....

....

....

....

....

Witnesses.. Signed ....

....

Terrier, whose standing in the eyes of the general public was precarious at least. Times had changed from the days of acceptability of bull and bear baiting, and those who fought dogs for sport and monetary gain – along with their dogs – were regarded with much suspicion and mistrust. In the years between 1850 and 1870, a period when dog breeding had begun to be taken very seriously, the 'Staffordshire Bull Terrier to be' was scarcely considered due to his reputation as a type of dog not to be encouraged. With the final legal demise of organised dog fighting and animal baiting finally brought about by the Protection of Animals Act of 1911, the Bull and Terrier as a breed might well have gradually disappeared. However, it was in the hearts and homes of those who really understood and appreciated the virtues of his temperament and love for people that he not only survived, but positively thrived.

To a great extent, the Staffordshire Bull Terrier (as he was later called) had always been a working man's constant pal and companion, especially so in the south Staffordshire Black Country area. From his background, this dog was undoubtedly a born fighter, but outside of the pit and in ordinary life, he was a docile and very intelligent companion. He had, despite his fighting background, earned his place in the societies of the miners, ironworkers and chain-makers of Staffordshire and other localities. He had become the family dog and guardian of the children, particularly in the Black Country area of Staffordshire where he was coveted and fully appreciated.

The breeders of this dog carefully preserved his characteristics along selective lines of breeding, which contributed to his eventual recognition as a pedigree dog. He used to be taken along to their workplace in the foundries and factories by his bosses, and was treated with great love and reverence by his families, who pampered him as much as they could in those poverty stricken days of the Industrial Revolution of the 19th century. Underground fighting and

Head study of a Staffordshire Bull Terrier c 1890.

matching of these dogs still continued, and a few resulting pounds earned by a working man at the end of a week in those hard times could well have made the difference between his family being well fed or not in the following week.

ESTABLISHING A BREED

Back in the period of the late 1920s, and in the well-established areas of the breed, things began to change for what was to become a total transformation for the dog himself. Devotees of the breed had come to realise the potential

of the dog they so cherished, and they started to make representations to the English Kennel Club with a view to recognition of pedigree status for the breed. This was not an easy task, due to the dog's previously considered dubious reputation. However, the tremendous efforts made in 1932 and 1933 by people like the actor Tom Wall, Count V.C. Hollander and, without doubt, Joseph Dunn and Joe Mallen paved the way forward. Towards the end of 1934, enthusiasts held a series of meetings with a view to forming a breed club. Such meetings culminated in May 1935 with over 40 breeders attending a meeting at the Old Crossguns Hotel, Cradley Heath in the Black Country, where Joe Mallen was the landlord.

The momentous day of that meeting saw the official naming of the breed. Attempts to include 'original' in the name had not met with Kennel Club approval, and what had been the Bull and Terrier or Pit dog was now officially named the 'Staffordshire Bull Terrier'– a fitting tribute to the historical and traditionally geographical location of the birth of the breed. The parent and first club of the breed was formed and named The Staffordshire Bull Terrier Club with Joseph Dunn appointed the first secretary. This pioneer had probably done more to see

THE FIRST SHOWS

Joseph Dunn set out to test the response to the new breed by organising shows early in 1935. The first show held on the bowling green of the Conservative Club at Cradley Heath was a great success and attracted an entry of 27 Staffords. The first club show was held on 17 August 1935 at Cradley Heath where 60 dogs and bitches were entered. These early shows proved to be very popular and attracted entries from far and wide. Feelings often ran high, and it was not unknown for skirmishes to take place between dogs or owners in those early days.

A landmark in the show history of the breed was at Crufts in 1936 where Staffords were shown for the very first time at this prestigious event. Joseph Dunn was fittingly appointed the judge for that day, and he awarded the best of breed to Joe Mallen's Cross Guns Johnson. Kennel Club registrations needed to reach a total of 750 for the breed to obtain Championship status in the show world. This was accomplished towards 1938, and the first Challenge Certificates for the breed were on offer at the Birmingham National Championship show in 1938. Mr A. Demaine awarded the first ever such prestigious awards to A. Boxley's dog Vindictive Montyson and to Joseph Dunn's bitch Lady Eve.

Championship shows were to follow at Crufts, Cheltenham and Bath, and it was at the Bath show when A.W. Fulwood awarded the third and final Challenge Certificates that make up to the title of Champion to the first ever Staffordshire Bull Terriers. The titles went to Joe Mallen's Champion Gentleman Jim and Joseph Dunn's Champion Lady Eve. The other Champions to be made up before the commencement of the war years of 1939 to 1945 were W.A. Boylan's Ch. Game Laddie; Miss A. Harrison's Ch. Madcap Mischief; and Mrs M. Beare's Ch. Midnight Gift.

Ch. Gentleman Jim: The first male Champion, made up in 1939.

Joe Mallen, pioneer of the breed, pictured with Stowcote Pride and a fighting cock.

through the establishment of the breed than any other.

The first Standard for the new pedigree breed, showing little difference from that currently in force except for the changes in height, was drawn up by the very people present who really knew what the Staffordshire Bull Terrier should be. Shaw's Jim (Jim the Dandy) and Peg's Joe (Fearless Joe) were the Staffords chosen as the representatives of the breed for this purpose. So here was a pedigree dog that epitomised the character of the Black Country, and bore by the very nature of his name, the region's geographical location on his broad shoulders.

WORLDWIDE FAME

The war years, as with that of all breeds, clearly curtailed the progress of the Staffordshire Bull Terrier in the show ring. It was therefore left open to speculation as to what those first great Champions and show Staffords, such as Ch. Gentleman Jim with his charismatic owner Joe Mallen, could have achieved during those years. However, popularity of the breed was spreading and Kennel Club registrations for the breed had risen from the modest annual total up to 1935 of 147 to an annual total 13 years later of 2,211 in the recorded registrations in the year of the

first change of the Kennel Club Standard for the breed in 1948. The numbers of Staffordshire Bull Terrier clubs and societies were also increasing. As long ago as 1937 had seen the formation of the Southern Counties Staffordshire Bull Terrier Society, and other areas of Britain were steadily becoming represented by the formation of Staffordshire Bull Terrier clubs and societies until they reached their current total of 18.

The fame of the breed was spreading everywhere. People leaving Britain to live in other countries of the world took their Staffords with them, and these dogs became established as family pets and show dogs with full recognition by the kennel clubs of those countries. The breed has succeeded and flourished to a remarkable extent throughout the world. It is well established in the United States of America, and, following recognition by the American Kennel Club, the breed has risen to a most prominent position in the American show scene. With the aid of quality dogs and bitches imported from Britain, there are many first-class Staffords and enthusiastic, well-supported clubs that provide excellent support for lovers of the breed. Shows are well organised and much support is given by the well-established Staffordshire Bull Terrier clubs and relative media.

Sadly, the situation in parts of Canada is somewhat overshadowed at present by

The fame of the breed spread as people travelled away from Britain, taking their Staffordshire Bull Terriers with them.

unjustified discrimination of the whole breed due to breed-specific dangerous dogs legislation. Regretfully, it is this type of legislation that again, without justification, has for many years resulted in an almost complete collapse of the breed in Germany.

With regard to the rest of Continental Europe, the Staffordshire Bull Terrier is at the heights of popularity as both pet and show dog, and the breed has for many years been very well established in South Africa, Australia and New Zealand. All these countries of the world have well-established Staffordshire Bull Terrier structures that are recognised and supported by their relevant Kennel Clubs. Certainly times have changed in the worldwide establishment and progress of the Stafford.

Modern means of communication have had a dramatic and exciting contribution to the extent that the whole world now has access to all aspects of the breed. Show judges travel the world, and Staffords themselves are shown unimpeded across continents.

CURRENT STATUS

The status and popularity enjoyed today by the Staffordshire Bull Terrier comes at a price. British Kennel Club registrations in 2005 for the breed amounted to a staggering 13,070, to be followed in 2006 by 12,729. Clearly, over-breeding a popular dog is not in the best interests of those who respect responsibility for the breed. The rescue organisations are inundated with unwanted puppies, which have clearly been bred for gain by those who have no direct interest other than taking advantage of the popularity of the breed. Fortunately, there are many responsible breeders who maintain the traditional virtues and temperament of the Stafford by careful breeding along selective and proven lines. From these breeders puppies are produced who further the breed, and who are not a response to the advertising in the media.

Yes, the Staffordshire Bull Terrier has changed from those times back in 1935 to the dog we see today. Physically the main change, in order to balance the Stafford from the differing variations that had entered the breed, has come about by a reduction in the height clause in the 1935 Standard for the breed from 15 to 18 inches high at the shoulder, to 14 to 16 inches high at the shoulder in the 1949 Standard. That height requirement stands today. All other changes that have been made may be regarded as cosmetic for show presentation. The Stafford of today should otherwise adhere to the original requirements set out by the founders of the breed who knew only too well what a Stafford should be, except that

we now have a heavier-built dog per height than that of the fighting days. Clearly there has been some change to the temperament of the breed, with much of the necessary aggressiveness of the fighting dog of yesterday curtailed by

indifferent breeding or disciplined control.

A true and well-bred Stafford of today will still show what he can do if provoked, and it is doubtful if his true temperament of love for people and fearlessness in a fight will ever be entirely eliminated. Perhaps what those who really know and love the breed can so readily believe comes from the words of Joseph Dunn, the man who worked so hard to give us all the honour of owning a Staffordshire Bull Terrier.

"The man in the street asks only for a dog which will not disgrace him by running for a hare if another dog shows fight. But the dog that he has must have other attributes, and in addition mental characteristics which will make him in the true sense, a faithful companion.

"To my way of thinking, there are three such attributes which the ideal companion must possess. These are intelligence,

The Staffordshire Bull Terrier now has an international reputation as an outstanding show and companion dog.

The Stafford's fighting days are far behind him, and we now have a breed of impeccable temperament.

teach-ability and a willingness to please his owner by obeying him.

"The 'Stafford' has all of these".

The world has moved on from the days of Joseph Dunn and his fellow founders of the breed. With the new and exciting era of pedigree Staffordshire Bull Terriers came changes that the early sporting gentlemen who had bred the dogs for fighting would never have dreamed possible, or would never have desired to be possible. Fortunately for us all, one vitally clear and unmistakable attribute of the Staffordshire Bull Terrier has shone through to raise the stature of this game athlete of a dog into the hearts and homes of tens of thousands of people throughout the world. I refer, of course, to the unmistakeable, fabulous temperament of the Stafford and his total trust of human beings. A most loyal and true family dog, full of heart and dependability.

A STAFFORD FOR YOUR LIFESTYLE

3 Chapter

A dog can, and indeed should, be an important member of a family. Before we buy a piece of equipment for our homes we usually do some research. Unfortunately, people often buy a dog for their family with little or no real knowledge about the character and needs of the breed they choose. We select almost on a whim: an appealing advert on television catches our attention; we see a breed that looks beautiful at Crufts; a friend has one; we had one as a child. Too often, we fail to consider the most important issue: will this type of dog fit into our particular lifestyle?

The Staffordshire Bull Terrier is, on the face of it, an easy dog to maintain and one that should fit into any family. He is of medium size, has a short, easy-to-manage coat, a very strong constitution and loves people, especially children. However, adaptable as a Stafford is, he is not suitable for all families. A Stafford will not sit quietly in a corner; he is a fussy dog, craving attention and pats from anyone close at hand. He is not always tolerant of other animals. Although a Stafford may protect his own family members – especially the youngest and weakest – he is not a natural guard or watch dog. A Stafford will rarely bark, and will not be keen to guard the home when left without human companions. Most Staffords have a great deal of energy and greet visitors robustly. It therefore follows that, if you take a Stafford into your life, you must be willing to spend a great deal of time with him. He will not take kindly to being left for hours on his own, and is unlikely to do well in a kennel.

THE COMMITMENT

Taking any dog into your family means making a big commitment in time and expense. Taking on such a lively, human-dependent dog as the Stafford takes a special commitment.

First of all, you must take stock of your way of life and discuss with your family, frankly, what the dog's needs are and whether or not you will be able to supply those needs. You must be honest and realistic. For example, your teenage son might volunteer to walk the dog every single day, but you have to be absolutely sure that he will be able to sustain this promise. It is easier to keep a dog if some member of the family is at home for at least part of the day. If you are all working full-time, you will need to consider getting a friend or a member of your family to call in at least once a day to exercise and give attention to your Stafford. If a

Weigh up the pros and cons before taking on the commitment of owning a Staffordshire Bull Terrier.

CAR ADDICTS

As a point of interest, most Staffords love cars or, indeed, any vehicle. If you have a job that involves a lot of travel, you may well find it convenient to take your dog along. He should be secure within the vehicle, and be careful where you leave him, as Staffords are the most popular breed for 'dog nappers'. Of course, be careful in warm weather, as car interiors heat up quickly, which can be fatal to a dog.

Stafford is not given enough time, attention and exercise, he will become destructive – and, bearing in mind the strength of his jaws and teeth, this could have a devastating effect on your home and its contents.

There are now professional dog walkers who can help to look after your Stafford, but many of these professionals take a number of dogs for a walk at any one time. You need to be very sure that your Stafford is 'dog tolerant'. Alternatively, you should make arrangements for your Stafford to be exercised on his own. Staffords, like most dogs, appreciate a routine, and once you have organised a way to manage your work hours and the needs of the dog, he will readily adapt.

GROUND RULES

It is a good idea to lay down some 'ground rules' even before your puppy comes home. While a puppy is small, it is easy, and of little inconvenience, to let him go anywhere in the house – to sit on the furniture and maybe even sleep on your bed. However, you must remember that soon your Stafford will be big, and you may not want him to behave in this way. If you allow him to sit on furniture, he will want to do this whether his feet are clean or muddy. A sweet puppy curled up on your bed is very different to having a large, heavy adult Stafford fighting you for space! It is better to start as you mean to go on, and put a dog's bed or a duvet in front of the fire or a radiator – Staffords have short coats and do relish warmth.

Once you have decided where the pup will sleep, keep to it and make it a two-way process. Human members of the family should accept that that is the dog's space, and if he retires to his bed, he should be left alone to rest. This is particularly important where there are children in the house. Learning to behave responsibly towards a dog is a very important lesson for life for any child to learn.

You should also agree who will feed the dog, and where and when he should be fed. All the family should agree not to feed treats from the table to the dog. If need be, train your dog to go and sit in his bed during family meal times.

A SUITABLE HOME

A Stafford does not need a large house or acres of garden to be happy, but he does need a fully fenced garden or enclosed yard. Ideally, your Stafford should have free access to a garden, and it will also make house training far easier if he has ready access to a safe, outside area.

If you live in a city, the majority of your dog's exercise will be in public parks. It is most important that you protect a young Stafford from any possible bullies in the park. If a young Stafford has a bad beating when he is young, he will never forget this and could well turn into a dog-intolerant adult.

When he is full grown, you must be careful that your Stafford does not become a bully himself.

The Stafford is a dog to be reckoned with, and it is your responsibility to keep him under control at all times.

Keep him under control at all times. Try using an extending lead or keep him on a short lead if you are moving among a number of strange dogs. Unfortunately, people can be very inconsiderate, and all Stafford owners have met the 'he doesn't mean it – he won't hurt your dog' type of owner, as a large mutt hurtles towards your now bristling Stafford.

If you live in the country, your opportunities for free exercise are, of course, greater. But there are different sorts of dangers lurking. The chief of these is the danger of your dog disappearing into a field of livestock, such as sheep or cows. The animals will immediately start to run, which will prove too tempting for any self-respecting Stafford – and the results could be disastrous. Train your Stafford to come to heel as

COUNTING THE COST

Even a dog as strongly constructed as a Stafford is expensive to maintain. Your dog will need good-quality food, regular inoculations, and possibly other veterinary attention from time to time. Sometimes a Stafford will be up for rehoming simply because the owners have failed to take account of the extra burden that keeping a dog can place on the family finances. You might consider taking out insurance against veterinary treatment so that you are not faced with large, unexpected bills.

The best scenario is to take your Stafford away on holiday, but this is not always possible.

you approach a field that has livestock, or keep him on the lead until the danger passes. It is also advisable to know the area where you are walking. Behind a hedge there may be a road – and too many Staffords have lost their lives to an unexpected car on a road. To maintain complete safety, children should never be allowed to exercise an adult Stafford unless accompanied by an adult.

CHANGES IN THE FAMILY

It is important to consider changes that might occur in your family during the lifetime of your dog. A new baby or an elderly relative coming into your family alters the whole scenario. Staffords, in general, are very tolerant of children and usually show the elderly remarkably tender care.

If you feel that you do not wish to share your new baby's life with an animal, please don't buy a dog until after you have had your family. I should add that when properly introduced, a Stafford and a baby are great companions – and I speak from experience. Hygiene is, of course, extra important here. I always keep dog-eating utensils completely separate from those used by humans, washing and drying them with their own cloths, even when there are no children in the household.

HOLIDAYS

A particular problem is what to do with your Staffordshire Bull Terrier while you are on holiday. It may be that you have a relation or a friend who will offer to keep him – maybe you can arrange a reciprocal arrangement with their dog. This can be a very acceptable arrangement, but it can also result in absolute tragedy. If your dog is taken out of his own home, it is of the utmost importance that you ensure the new temporary home is completely dog safe. What might be a safe fence for most breeds of dogs could well be completely unsafe for a Stafford. A Stafford is more than capable of punching his way through the thickest and prickliest of hedges, or jumping over high fences if he is really determined. Disasters arising from a Stafford breaking out of a strange home are common, and very distressing for all concerned.

The safest place to leave your Stafford is a good boarding kennel. Personal recommendation – especially from another Stafford owner – is the best way to find a suitable establishment. Staffords do not make the easiest guests – they often cannot mix with the other boarders and they pine for their own home and family. To overcome this latter problem, it is far the best policy to start your Stafford in kennels for short periods while he is young. If he goes on to have regular visits to the kennel – once or twice a year – he is far more likely to settle and flourish.

Speaking as a retired boarding kennel owner, there is nothing sadder than seeing an elderly dog, who has never experienced the noise and bustle of a busy boarding kennel, trying to come to terms with his new surroundings for the first time. A good boarding kennel will require up-to-date inoculations and possibly ask for protection against kennel cough (see Chapter 8: Happy and Healthy).

Alternatively, you can pay for home sitters to look after your pets, which has the added bonus of having your home cared for as well. Make sure that you forbid any such sitter from letting your Stafford off the lead when on their walks together. Again, personal recommendation is by far the best method of recruiting.

MALE OR FEMALE?

Choosing the sex of your Stafford very much depends on your lifestyle. A bitch is usually slightly smaller, lighter and quieter than the average male. However, she will have a twice-yearly heat or season, and unless you have a fully fenced garden you will be bothered by strange dogs coming calling, or by your bitch taking off to find her own mate. If you do not intend to breed from your

The male Stafford is bigger and heavier than the female, and may be more aggressive.

If you choose a bitch, you will have to contend with twice-yearly seasons unless she is neutered.

Stafford bitch, it is advisable to have her neutered. Consult your vet for advice.

A male Stafford is larger, heavier and is generally more aggressive towards other animals than a bitch, although this is mainly dependant on his level of dominance. Given a firm hand and plenty of activity, however, a male Stafford is a fun-loving, entertaining companion for your family. If you already have a dog, of whatever breed, it is better to choose a Stafford of the opposite sex. It is particularly difficult to get two male Staffords to agree once they reach maturity. In general it is best to buy only one dog of whatever sex at a time – rearing two puppies together is certainly more than double the trouble.

FINDING A PUPPY

Once you have done your research and thought really seriously about your choice of breed, the next problem is where to obtain your puppy. It is always best to buy a dog from a breeder rather than a commercial outlet. Deciding who is and who is not a reputable, experienced breeder, is not easy. In Staffords it would

HEALTH CHECKS

There are health checks related to inherited disease in the Staffordshire Bull Terrier. The Stafford now has two DNA tests available to avoid the production of animals affected by the conditions: hereditary juvenile cataracts (HC) and L-2- hydroxyglutaric aciduria (L-2HGA).

You should ensure the status of the parents of the litter for these DNA tests, plus they should have had an eye test for persistent hyperplastic primary vitreous (PHPV), for which, unfortunately, there is no DNA test as yet.

Note the difference between being affected by one of these conditions and being a carrier for one of them. A carrier is, in no way, an unhealthy animal as far as ordinary living is concerned. Its carrier status only becomes of importance if you decide to breed from him or her. If both the

parents of your puppy are carriers for one of these conditions, there is a chance that your puppy could become affected and this will exhibit itself when he is older and you have become attached to him. If only one of the parents is a carrier, then your puppy will not be affected but may be a carrier itself. If someone mates a litter from a carrier to a clear (non-carrier), I would expect them to have all the puppies tested so that you will know the status of your puppy. If both of the parents of your puppy are 'clear' (i.e. non-carriers), then your puppy will neither be affected nor be a carrier.

From the above, I think you will see how important it is that the breeder has taken the responsible action of ascertaining the genetic status of the dogs he has mated. (For more information on inherited diseases, see Chapter 8.)

It is important to establish how the puppies have been reared, as this will have an effect on how well socialised they are.

appear that the experience of a breeder is in inverse proportion to the amount of advertising he/she undertakes. It would seem that the more experienced and more successful breeders have less necessity to advertise their stock. The best method to track down a good breeder is to approach your local breed club (see Appendices) or to go through the official Stafford club websites on the internet. In addition, it is a good idea to take one of the recognised dog papers and go to one of the shows that are advertised. Here you can mix with many Staffords and talk to their owners and breeders. You will have a chance to see how the dogs behave towards their owners and other dogs. You can also see

the colours of the Stafford at first hand.

When you have located a litter for sale or ascertained that a breeder is likely to be having a litter, you should make a few enquiries. First and foremost, both parents and the litter should be registered with the appropriate national Kennel Club. Having a pedigree is nothing more than a few names on a piece of paper unless it is backed up with papers from the Kennel Club. The 'official' Kennel Club in the UK is located in London, with its registration department in Aylesbury. It should not be confused with any other so-called 'Kennel Club' operating from someone's front room!

REARING STRATEGY

You should ask any breeder you contact about the number of puppies in the litter, and how they have been reared. It is best for any Stafford puppy to start life in the house. Such puppies will have been introduced to the noises of the house: television, music, vacuum cleaner, washing machine, etc. at a very early age. A home-reared puppy is more likely to have been much handled by the breeder's family and to be well socialised.

If a litter has been kennel-reared, you will need to assure yourself that the puppies have been given sufficient play time and contact with all members of a family.

You might also ascertain how many of the litter have already been sold. Do not be deterred when there is only one left – unless it is an obvious runt. There is many a well-known winning adult that was the puppy everyone overlooked when selecting from the litter.

COLOURS

You may have already decided that you would prefer a specific colour. Black brindles are by far the most numerous of Staffords. However, there is a wide range of brindles from silver grey to red (mahogany) brindle. Wholly red or the paler fawn Staffords are not as numerous, but are still readily available. Pied or skewbald

The puppies should look bright-eyed, alert, and interested in everything that is going on around them.

Staffords – that is either white with brindle, or white with red or fawn – are very popular. Blue is not a particularly rare colour, although it is not regularly seen in the show ring because blues often come with yellow eyes and slate noses, which are not desirable according to the Breed Standard (see Chapter 7: The Perfect Stafford). You should be careful when selecting a blue, as many of these may appear a slate blue in the nest but become a mushroom colour as an adult. You should never pay extra for a so-called 'rare' colour.

BUYER BEWARE!

The most attractive feature of a Stafford is his temperament. It is therefore important that you see as many of the pups' relatives as you can – and especially the mother. If there are any restrictions on seeing the dam of a litter, I would be suspicious.

Seeing the sire might be another matter. People who are breeding to improve their stock, as opposed to those who are merely breeding litters for financial gain, are most likely to travel, often a long way, to find a suitable mate for their bitch. If you go to a dog show, you may be able to view the stud dog that has been used. Otherwise, beware of the breeder with half a dozen

KEEPING IT CLEAN

It is more important than you might think for the puppies to have clean living quarters. From an early age, Stafford puppies will attempt to crawl away from their sleeping area to relieve themselves. A good rearing set-up will therefore have a sleeping area and a playing/toileting area. The sooner a pup concerns himself with cleanliness, the easier he will be to house train. Indeed, in my experience, puppies that have been allowed to wallow in dirty conditions often grow into adults who are unreliable about cleanliness in the house.

bitches all mated to their own, usually unshown, stud dog. These pups have most likely been bred for money. Such puppies may be fine, but, then again, they may not be. You are also less likely to have a good 'after sales' service as you are from a recognised breeder who has a reputation to maintain among his peers.

If you go to a well-established breeder, even if you are not able to meet the father, you might well be able to meet uncles, aunts or other relations, as well as the mother, and this will help to build up a picture of the family you are buying into.

Try to see more than one litter, and if anything strikes you as not quite right, don't be afraid to say you will think it over and then go to see another litter. Do not be bulldozed into leaving a deposit on a puppy.

On the other hand, you should

be prepared to answer questions from the breeder about your intentions and the quality of life you are able to offer the puppy. Indeed, if the only concern of the breeder is getting hold of your money, I would not call them a responsible breeder.

CHOOSING A STAFFORD

Before you choose a puppy, you need to be clear in your own mind as to what you want from your Staffordshire Bull Terrier. This will have a major bearing on what you are looking for.

A PET PUPPY

If you want a Stafford purely as a companion, the most important considerations are temperament, health checks of the parents, and the healthy rearing of the puppies. The puppies' living accommodation should be clean, and they should be parasite-free. Avoid puppies with bloated stomachs, which could be indicative of worms. You might check that the pup does not have an umbilical hernia – a poppy 'belly button' – which is not uncommon on a Stafford. An abdominal hernia will almost certainly disappear as the puppy grows, but you might check that it can be pushed back gently with your fingers, and the breeder should point this out to you.

Inguinal hernias in the groin are very rarely seen in the breed.

Look for bright eyes, shiny coats and, above all, a willingness to come up to greet you with tails wagging. Make sure that the mother is friendly, and that the pups are being fed a sensible diet. You should be offered a full diet sheet if and when you buy a puppy. (For more information on feeding, see Chapter 5: The Best of Care.)

The physical condition of the dam might also give you a clue as to the general good management of the breeder. You should expect the mother to be somewhat thinner than usual, especially if she has reared a large litter. But her undercarriage should not be over-stretched as if the puppies have been allowed to suckle from her for too long. Keeping puppies suckling for many weeks on the

mother is a way of cutting down on the expense of buying food to wean the puppies, and is, of course, far less time-consuming!

Ideally, puppies should leave their mother at around eight weeks of age. They should never leave before six weeks old, as such puppies have not had time to develop enough independence from their mother and littermates, and they are being deprived of the protection from disease that they gain from even small feeds from their mother.

A SHOW PUPPY
You may have decided that you want to exhibit your puppy when he grows up. In other words, you are hoping to buy a 'show' dog. Now this, with any breed, is a difficult assignment. With a Stafford it is particularly difficult, as successful show dogs are very

hard to produce. Consider that in any one year in the UK, there are approximately 13,000 Stafford puppies registered, and yet the average number of Staffords that make it to Champion is only about 12 annually.

If you are determined to buy a show dog, ask an experienced breeder or exhibitor to go with you to view the puppies. No breeder worth his salt will guarantee that an eight-week-old puppy will make a show dog; all they can do is show you the most promising pups in the litter. When choosing a puppy that may turn out to be a show dog, you should look for temperament and health just as for the companion dog but, in addition, you must evaluate the make and shape of the pup.

The one part of the pup that will change least is the head. A long, weak head with a poor stop at six weeks old will not turn into a well-shaped, strong head at 16 months. You should look for a head where the eyes are wide set and the ears fairly low on the side of the pup's skull. There should also be a well-defined 'stop', and some strength through the foreface.

Size and substance are more unpredictable and depend to some extent on the quality of the food and the general husbandry you give the pup. However, you should look for a squarely made, short-backed and upstanding puppy; one that moves freely with rather well-bent hindquarters. The teeth should be in a scissor bite, with the teeth

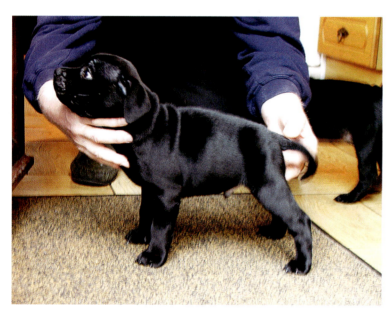

The breeder will help you to assess which puppies have show potential.

on the upper jaw closely overlapping the teeth on the lower jaw. The pup should be substantial without being over fat. Puppies will quickly refine as they become more active, so a finely built, willowy pup is not the best to choose.

You should also make yourself familiar with the colours permitted by the Breed Standard. Studying the colours given in the registration of some puppies, e.g. 'champagne', 'chocolate' etc, proves that some 'breeders' are not familiar with the recognised colours for the breed. If you don't do your homework, you may come home with a pretty 'chocolate' Stafford that is unsuitable for showing.

Depending on the age at which you first see the litter, you might find red puppies showing an amount of black hair on their bodies, but this will clear as they grow older. Black masks, on the other hand, are acceptable at any age. Very young pied puppies might exhibit 'butterfly noses' (noses that are part pink and part black). Such a nose should be totally black by about eight weeks. It is worth noting that after eight weeks, because parts of the pup will develop at different rates, he may not retain the exact, balanced shape he had at seven weeks. However, the original qualities should return from around six months of age onwards.

It is worth noting that on more than one occasion, a complete novice has bought a so-called pet who turned out to be a big-

You made decide that it is better for you to take on an older dog.

winning Champion. In fact, Stafford enthusiasts through the years have been proud of the open nature of the competition within the breed.

Perhaps a safer way to find a show dog is to buy an older puppy or young adult. Sometimes breeders will need to part with such an animal if they are overstocked. You may not be able to buy a Champion in this way, but you could certainly buy an animal you could show and expect to have some success with.

AN OLDER DOG
Looking for an adult dog as a companion offers many advantages. Providing that the animal has been kept in the house, you are saved the problems of house training. Such a dog should be over the 'chewing' stage, which usually occurs when the pup is changing his teeth. An older dog may know some commands, such as Sit, and Stay; he may be lead trained and may have some knowledge of the world.

REHOMING ORGANISATIONS

There are nationwide rehoming organisations that advertise widely and there are also rescue organisations specifically for Staffords. A list of these organisations can be from the Kennel Club, and each one listed is officially sponsored by a breed club.

A good rescue organisation will spend a lot of time quizzing you as to your home conditions and will also give you a home-check. This involves someone with a good knowledge of the breed visiting your home and assuring themselves that, on the practical level, you have a safe and suitable home for a Stafford, and that you understand the character of the breed.

The aim is to match a dog to a new home. For example, an older dog that has never lived with children would not necessarily be suitable to go to a house with four or five lively youngsters running around. Rescue organisations normally spay bitches and some castrate dogs.

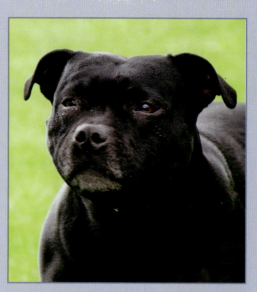

The aim is to match dog and owner to ensure that rehoming is successful.

There are several possibilities for you to source an adult dog. Breeders very often run on puppies only to find they develop some fault or lack certain virtues, which make them unsuitable for showing. Keeping a large number of Staffords is very difficult, as you cannot give them the time they need for playing, walking and petting. Therefore, many breeders will look for a good home for a young adult who has not come up to scratch, or for a young bitch who has produced a litter and will not be used for breeding again.

There are also many rescue organisations that work tirelessly on behalf of the Staffordshire Bull Terrier. People who run these organisations are often inundated with unwanted or simply discarded Staffords. The plight of these dogs – most of whom are perfectly normal, good-tempered animals – is, at the present time, quite desperate. Popularity of the breed has encouraged excessive breeding, and all too often owners have acquired a Stafford in haste only to find the dog unsuitable for their lifestyle.

RESCUED DOGS

Most rescued dogs are just animals that have fallen on hard times. Perhaps their owners have become ill or have had to relocate to places where dogs are not allowed. Many dogs are the innocent victims of family breakdowns. Too often, it is just a case of the owners moving on to a more fashionable breed. Occasionally dogs have problems, which are usually caused by lack of proper training, or even the wrong kind of training. Saddest of all are dogs who have suffered cruelty

It takes time, patience and dedication to help a rescued dog to settle into a new home.

from their previous owners – such as the young dog set alight and 'posted' down a refuse shute in a block of flats. Some dogs come into rescue having been found wandering in the street, and then there is no history to help the rescuers place them.

If you take on one of these dogs, you may need a great deal of patience. You may find the Stafford has unusual fears, he may be destructive in the house, disobedient when out for walks, or aggressive with other dogs. You need to be patient and spend time with your Stafford, and perhaps even seek specialist help. Some may need long-term veterinary attention. If you have the time and patience, there is an undoubted reward for you in the trust and understanding you will build up between the dog and yourself.

For owners of rescued dogs it is a deeply moving experience if, after days, weeks, even months of working with a dog, trying endless ways of gaining his trust, or trying to teach a new behaviour, suddenly the problem is solved, the 'penny drops' and you have achieved yet one more step towards good behaviour. This is a most rewarding experience, and one you will never forget.

THE NEW ARRIVAL

4
Chapter

'Start as you mean to go on' is the best advice available. Unruly puppies may be a source of entertainment, but it is not so amusing when the same unwanted behaviour is displayed by a fully-grown adult Staffordshire Bull Terrier. So decide upon the house rules and stick to them; it may be very difficult at times, but it will pay off in the long term. This also applies to an adult rescued animal who may have been given little or no previous discipline.

Once you have decided that the Staffordshire Bull Terrier is the dog for you, sit down with the family and make the decisions as to where the dog will sleep, how and when he is to be exercised, and what and when he is to be fed. It is down to you to ensure that he becomes a well-behaved and well-adjusted part of the family.

SAFETY IN THE HOME

Prior to obtaining your new mini bulldozer, ensure that everything necessary has been done to make his new home safe. Puppies in particular are naturally inquisitive and will investigate any new object by smelling or chewing it, so simple precautions should be taken to prevent damage or injury to him. Remove any breakable items and try not to leave any small objects lying about. Shoes and slippers, children's toys and electric wiring are irresistible to a youngster and are therefore best kept out of reach. Even a seemingly harmless object can be a potential killer if eaten.

Keep outside doors and windows closed to prevent your puppy wandering and restrict access to any area in the home that could prove to be a danger to him. This is where a stairgate may prove to be invaluable in securing the safety of your new addition.

Staffords are very keen gardeners and no stone will be left unturned when your puppy is given the chance to investigate. A youngster may be irresistibly drawn to the garden pond but it may prove fatal. Make sure that ponds and swimming pools are covered at first, or deny him access to the area until he learns better. It is also imperative that the garden is securely fenced and that any gaps are filled and made safe. Gates should be kept closed at all times and preferably locked while not in use – many a Stafford has been tragically involved in a traffic accident because a gate has been left open. Staffords are also a target for thieves, so never leave your puppy outside unattended.

There are also a number of plants that are not dog-friendly, and some have poisonous bark or seed pods that may prove fatal to a puppy. If you are unsure of

Stafford puppies love to explore, so you will need to check your home for potential hazards.

which plants are toxic, a little research on the subject may be in order – the internet has a wealth of information on the subject or ask your local garden centre for advice. Be aware that slug pellets and weed killers both pose a great danger to dogs. If you have to use a weed killer, purchase one that it is animal-friendly.

BUYING EQUIPMENT

CRATE/DOG BED

All dogs need their own quiet place to which they can retire without being disturbed. Puppies in particular need their own place to sleep. A crate/indoor kennel, which must match the size of the dog, may prove to be invaluable as long as it is used sensibly and only for reasonably short periods of time. A puppy will soon make this his personal space. If you line the crate floor with newspaper, it will help with house training (see page 59). The puppy can also be in the midst of activity while in the security of his cage, and will still be safe even if you have to leave the room. Staffords will often choose to sleep overnight in the crate with the door left open, as long as comfortable bedding is provided. The best type of bedding to buy is synthetic fleece, which is machine-washable and dries quickly.

If you wish to provide a bed for elsewhere in the home, the best type to buy is a tough, plastic, kidney-shaped model. These are easier to clean and harder for a dog to damage. Line the base with comfortable bedding, which should be washed and changed frequently.

BOWLS

Access to clean water should be made available at all times. If you decide to use a crate, it is best to purchase water bowls that clip on to the sides, preventing water spillage. Good-quality feeding bowls should be provided. These come in many shapes and sizes, and each dog should have its own food bowl, which should always be kept clean. A heavy ceramic bowl or a rubber-rimmed stainless steel bowl are preferable, as these are less likely to move while the dog is eating.

A crate is an excellent investment.

GROOMING GEAR

Staffordshire Bull Terriers need very little in the way of grooming – just a few minutes a day. Use a good-quality bristle brush to groom the fine coat close to the skin or you may find that a grooming mitt that has fine rubber nodules on it fits the bill. Many Staffords also enjoy a bath but this should not be too often, as the natural oils in the coat may be destroyed. Always make sure that a good brand of special dog shampoo is used.

COLLAR AND LEAD

You will initially need a puppy collar that can be adjusted as the puppy grows. You may prefer to purchase the cheaper nylon collars for your puppy, who will probably outgrow a number of these before he reaches maturity. The adult Stafford will need a good-quality, standard one-inch (2.5 cm) wide leather collar with a matching lead of at least 6ft in length. A shorter lead gives less control, as the dog will tend to pull harder. A leather collar and lead set may prove a little expensive, but it will pay off in the long run and will often last for the animal's lifetime and beyond.

You may also wish to invest in a good-quality extending lead. Make sure that it is made of one-inch wide (2.5 cm) webbing and not the thin cord type, as these can be very hard on the fingers should you decide to reel it in quickly. As long as the lead is kept to a shorter length when walking your dog in built-up areas, an extending lead allows the dog a little more freedom while you are still in control.

Choke chains should definitely be avoided, as a Stafford is likely to pull against the restraint. This may cause severe chaffing or affect his breathing. Likewise a chain link is not recommended. This type of lead is far too heavy and less flexible; also the noise of it may be enough to unnerve or distract your dog.

Many Stafford owners prefer to use a harness, but please be aware that you have far less control over your dog than when he is wearing a collar. If you must use a harness, try the padded nylon type along with a collar and tag.

FINDING A VET

Obviously you need your vet to be within a viable distance, which narrows your search somewhat. However, the priority is to find a vet who offers the best-quality care to his patients. Ask around your friends and neighbours for their recommendation, providing that you are happy to trust their judgement.

ID

It is advised that all dogs wear an identity disc attached to the collar. This should always be worn when out in a public place and should display your contact details. It is also a good idea to have your dog microchipped. This procedure can be performed by a vet, or by a registered charity that may offer the service. The microchip provides a permanent identity number that can be scanned and is extremely effective in reuniting a lost pet with his owners.

TOYS

Finding safe toys for a Staffordshire Bull Terrier is a hard task, as they are very strong chewers. Puppies in particular are prone to chewing and safe toys need to be provided. The best option is to buy hard rubber toys, such as Kongs or Boomer Balls. The adult Stafford may also appreciate the larger size Galileo bones: these fray slightly and help a little with cleaning the teeth. They also have a meaty taste and can be boiled to refresh and cleanse.

Staffords also love a good game of tug, but be sure that your dog is willing to let go when you ask him to; if not, ignore him until he is ready to play it your way. Do not provide your Stafford with soft or squeaky toys, as they are easily destroyed and may prove fatal if swallowed.

COLLECTING YOUR PUPPY

At last it is time for you to collect your puppy. This is an exciting day for you and your family, but a very confusing time for the puppy. Moving home can be a very traumatic experience, even for this, the most confident of breeds.

When you arrive home let your puppy investigate his new surroundings, but stay with him so that he does not become afraid of any new sights or sounds. Remember that your puppy is leaving the security of the only environment that he has ever known. He will have to live without the warmth and comfort of his mother and littermates, and he will have to get used to an entirely new routine. Introduce him preferably at a time when the house is quiet so

Stafford pups will enjoy a variety of toys, but as your pup grows bigger you will need to buy tougher, rubber toys.

that he has the time to settle in without too much fuss. Give him the chance to explore both the house and garden, but do be on hand to reassure him when necessary.

MEETING THE FAMILY

Staffords love children – hence their popularity with young families. But mutual respect is the key. When the puppy first arrives home, provide the children with alternative entertainment, such as a game or a new video, which will help to lessen the interest caused by the new addition. This gives the puppy a better chance to settle in and get to know everyone gradually.

Children must be made aware that the new arrival is not the latest toy and that the pup must be allowed his own space. The children also need to learn how to be fair yet firm, ignoring the puppy if he becomes too excited, and giving him the chance to control his enthusiasm. A quiet place should be provided for the puppy where he can sleep undisturbed. This should be a no-go area for the children, who must learn to leave him alone when he needs to rest.

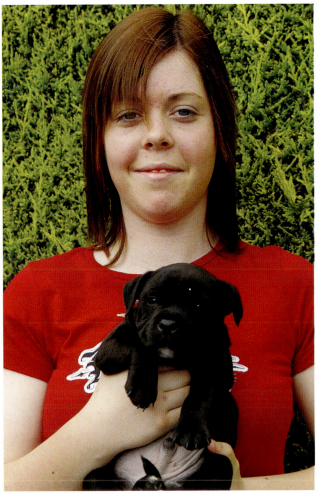

The puppy needs to be taught the difference between a child and his littermates; a young puppy's teeth are very sharp and a playful nip can be quite painful. Sit the children down on the floor prior to them handling the pup. A Stafford pup is very strong and can easily wriggle free from a child's arms, often with severe consequences, such as a broken limb. The correct way to

The waiting is over, and it is time to take your puppy home.

handle a puppy is to have one hand under his bottom and the other between his front legs, helping to restrain him.

If you don't have children of your own, it is very important that the puppy meets and has fun with children of all ages during his early months. This should always be under adult supervision, particularly where toddlers are concerned, as a boisterous puppy could easily knock a toddler over. If need be, encourage the puppy towards the child with a treat or his favourite toy. If the pup is overly excitable, try to calm him a little prior to offering the treat. Rewarding his calmness may encourage him to be a little less boisterous in future.

There is nothing that your new Stafford puppy will love better than a good game, but if the children become too excited then the puppy will get excited, too. Do not let your puppy get away with doing anything to your children that would not be acceptable from an adult dog. This includes chasing and jumping up, particularly if he has the inclination to grab clothing. Most puppies will chase anything that moves, so nip this tendency

If relations get off to a good start, your Stafford will soon be an integral member of the family.

in the bud and teach him that playing with his own toys is much more fun.

MEETING THE FAMILY PETS
Similar rules apply when introducing your new puppy to other pets. Most adult Staffords will happily accept a young puppy, particularly if it is the opposite sex. Introduce the dog at the earliest opportunity, and keep

them under constant supervision until you are sure that they have accepted each other. It is likely that a game will be next on the agenda, but be sure to put an end to it when enough is enough, as the puppy will be unlikely to know when to stop.

Introduce your puppy to small pets, such as rabbits, hamsters, guinea pigs etc, while he is on the lead so that he cannot chase

them. Familiarity breeds contempt, and the pup should become bored after a time. If you have no other pets then try taking him to visit friends who have, so that he can be socialised with different animals.

Many Staffords live quite happily with the family cat, but it is vital to supervise initial meetings. In most cases, it is the cat that is the biggest cause for

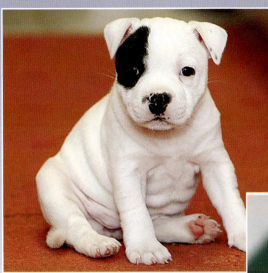

When a puppy arrives in his new
home, there is so much to take in.

After a period of
exploring, he will
need a chance to rest.

concern, as she is able to inflict a
nasty scratch on an unsuspecting
puppy. To begin with, never leave
the cat and puppy alone together
and make sure that the cat has an
escape route. If the puppy gives
chase or barks at the cat, tell him
"No" very firmly each time he
tries his luck, and reward him
when he responds to you.
Patience is definitely required,
but the time spent teaching him

how to behave will eventually pay
off, and in most cases your cat
and your Stafford will live
together in harmony.

SETTLING IN

MEAL TIMES
Most breeders will be happy to
supply a diet sheet with details of
how the puppy has been fed so
far. Some breeders will also

supply enough food to last for
several days. Do not be tempted
to change this until he has settled
in, as a change of diet can cause
severe tummy upsets.

Once the puppy is happy and
confident in his new
surroundings, you may decide
that his present diet is not what
you wish to feed. Should you
decide to make a change, make
sure you invest in the best-quality

THE FIRST NIGHT

stablish a routine so that when you put him to bed and turn out the light he knows it is time to sleep. If your puppy has been sleeping all evening, he is unlikely to be tired, so try playing with him for a while before he goes to bed. Try not to get him overly excited or he will be unlikely to settle down.

A puppy is quick to learn that if he cries during the night and you come to him, this is a good way of getting your attention. Try to resist his cries, unless he becomes very distressed, when you will want to stroke him and reassure him until he settles down. If your puppy fails to settle, you can try wrapping a warm hot-water bottle in a towel and placing it in his bed. The sound of a ticking alarm clock may remind him of his littermates' heartbeat may give him some comfort. If the puppy has taken well to a member of the family, then place an article of recently worn clothing in his bed.

As a last resort, you can take the puppy to your bedroom, but do not be tempted to let him on to your bed. A clever Stafford puppy will soon get used to the idea, but, remember, he will take up rather more space when he becomes an adult.

Accustom your puppy to his crate for short periods.

food that you can afford. A cheap diet may prove to be a false economy. If you decide upon a complete food, which provides everything your dog needs, it is preferable to feed one that has no colours or additives, which have been known to cause hyperactivity in Staffords. Introduce the new food gradually over a period of time (approximately six days), reducing his original diet slightly at each sitting and adding the same amount of the new diet until he is finally changed over to his new feeding regime. (For more information on feeding your Stafford, see Chapter 5: The Best of Care.)

A PLACE TO REST

Your puppy needs a quiet place to rest and sleep undisturbed. If you have decided to use a crate, accustom your puppy to it as soon as possible, as he will have been used to being confined in some way with the rest of the litter and will be more accepting of the situation.

Make sure that the crate is the right size for an adult Stafford – 61 cm by 46 cm by 53 cm (24 in by 18 in by 21 in) is usually the most suitable.

Place the cage in the chosen location, which should be draught-free. Make the crate cosy by lining it with bedding. Do not shut your Stafford in at first, as he may want to get up in the night to relieve himself. Once he is used to the crate, you may close the door for short periods of time, around 15 to 20 minutes, while you are still in the home. Gradually extend the time so that the puppy gets used to being on his own. If a puppy is taught from an early age that there are times when he has to be alone, there is less likelihood that he will become distressed when left for longer periods of time when he reaches adulthood. Your Stafford will see his crate as a safe place to go when he wants to rest. This is particularly important for a young, growing puppy who needs periods of sleep in order to grow happily and healthily.

Never use the crate to lock your Stafford away for hours on end. This is terribly cruel, particularly for a breed that is so people-motivated and that thrives on human attention.

HOUSE TRAINING

When your puppy wakes, he will want to relieve himself. Get yourself into the routine of going outside to the appropriate area and tell him to go, using the same command at all times. Once he has done what is expected of him, praise him greatly - this is a big achievement for one so young. Take your puppy out at regular intervals during the day: always when he wakes and usually after food or a play session where he may become excited and forget what he is supposed to do.

Never scold your puppy for making a mistake. The 'accident' may have happened some time previously, and the puppy will have no idea why he is being told off. If you find a mess, simply clean it up. It is best to use a solution of biological washing powder, as this removes the smell more thoroughly than disinfectants. If you catch your puppy in the act, encourage him to follow you outside so that he may complete his business, making sure that you praise him each time.

HOUSE RULES

'Start as you mean to go on' is never more important than when you are establishing house rules. If you don't want to share your furniture with your Stafford, now is the time to enforce the rules. Do not let him share the armchair with you, but, instead, place his bedding at your feet where he is

Take your puppy into the garden at regular intervals and he will soon learn what is required.

If your puppy becomes used to all-over handling, he will accept grooming and visits to the vet when he is older.

able to gain comfort from you. If you feel the need for a cuddle, sit on the floor with him.

There may be areas of the house where you do not want your Stafford to go. Again, be firm and consistent so that he understands the rules. The use of a stairgate to shut off these areas may prove to be invaluable.

MOUTHING

Mouthing is a common problem in puppies of all breeds – and Stafford puppies are no exception. This should be discouraged firmly but gently. If your pup tries to gain hold of your arm, tell him "No" every time so that he realises that you are displeased. If he continues

with this behaviour then withdraw your attention from him until he calms down a little. Some puppies may take longer to respond to this than others, but be patient and persevere, so that puppy mouthing does not become a bad habit in an adult dog.

EARLY LESSONS

Although your puppy is possibly still too young to be taken out for walks, you can introduce him to the collar and lead. A puppy is never too young to start learning as long as training sessions are short and full of fun.

Start by getting your puppy used to the collar for a short period, possibly just prior to a

meal time so that he has other things on his mind. The puppy may object to the collar initially, sitting down and refusing to move, or he may try scratching it. The best plan is to ignore such behaviour and only remove the collar when the puppy is not scratching, or he will feel that you have taken it off for that reason and may repeat the behaviour on subsequent occasions. Leave the collar on for slightly longer periods of time until your puppy gradually comes to accept it, but never leave it on when you are unable to supervise him, as this may lead to accidents. It is nothing unusual for a puppy to get tangled by his collar, so never take the risk.

When you are happy that your puppy has accepted his collar, try introducing him to the lead. Many puppies are averse to this at first, and some may take a real dislike to it, so you may need to be very patient. If your puppy tries to back off from you, do not be tempted to pull him back. Try to persuade him gently to come towards you, offering a treat or a favourite toy. Hopefully, the puppy will decide that this is of far more interest, in which case praise him greatly when he returns to you. Repeat this procedure until your Stafford is happy and confident enough to walk alongside you, remembering to praise him all the time.

YOUR PUP'S NEEDS

Caring for your puppy involves more than looking after his physical needs. You need to spend time with him, petting him and simply talking to him in order to establish a bond between you. Try to find some time every day to give him some one-to-one attention. A Stafford loves to have his tummy rubbed, and he will willingly come to you for a fuss. This will give you the opportunity to go over his body to check for any problems. You can also gently lift back his lips to examine his teeth and gums. Make these sessions pleasurable and you will soon gain your puppy's trust.

The first year of your Stafford's life is extremely important, as this is the time when he learns to respond to people and the world around him, so do try to give him as many positive experiences as possible. (For advice on socialisation, see Chapter Six.)

THE RESCUED DOG

Many of the problems of bringing up a new puppy may also apply to a rescued dog. But, of course, there are some pluses that may appeal to some owners. An adult Stafford will probably be able to be left for longer periods of time; he will generally be house trained, and used to a collar and lead. Most dogs that come through rescue do so

CAR TRAVEL

Although your new addition is not yet old enough to go outside, he may be taken out in the car. Start with short journeys, gradually increasing the length of time he spends in the car. Initially, car travel may make the puppy sick, so it is advisable to take him out on an empty stomach. Most pups soon become accustomed to travelling and will enjoy trips in the car. Make sure your puppy is secure in a crate or behind a dog guard. It is unwise to leave your Stafford in an unattended vehicle, as they are susceptible to theft and it is better not to take the risk. In warm weather, there is the health danger, too, of leaving a dog in a car. Many Staffords love to travel and may get quite excited, so always make sure that you secure your dog's lead before opening a car door, to avoid possible accidents.

through no fault of their own, possibly because of a breakdown in a relationship, a death or illness in the family, or simply a change of circumstances that does not allow for the dog to have a decent existence. However, it is important to be aware that some rescued dogs will have behavioural problems, which you should be made aware of prior to taking him on.

A breed rescue organisation is the first place to start. Being experienced in Staffordshire Bull Terriers they are more able to provide help and advice on the subject. In most cases they will be aware of the history of the dog, and will be prepared to talk you through the process prior to any decision. A home-check will be arranged to assess the

suitability of your house and garden, and to arrange the necessary paperwork. They will also insist that all rescued Staffords are neutered. The dog most suitable for your needs and circumstances will be the one to fit into your household. If you have children, it is best to choose a dog that has been bought up with a young family, as he is most likely to be more careful around them. The average Stafford lives for 12 to 15 years, so an older dog will still have a great deal to offer you, his new owners, and this is an option you may find well worth considering.

A NEW HOME

The length of time it takes for a rescued dog to settle in his new home largely depends on what he has been used to in the past. However, Staffordshire Bull Terriers are very keen to please, and if, once again, you start by enforcing your rules, most will be happy to comply. Being very people-motivated, Staffords enjoy nothing more than being in your company. A Stafford who is left to his own devices for too long will be easily bored and may become destructive. This is not the breed to take on if you are out of the house for long periods of time.

For the first few days, a rescued Stafford may not eat

very well; he will be unsettled and will need time to adjust to his new regime. Do not try to compensate by offering different types of food. If you know what he is used to eating, just persevere for a few days; he will eat when he is ready.

It is important that the rescued Stafford has his own place to sleep, so place his crate or bed in a suitable area where he will be undisturbed. He may have been allowed to climb on the furniture or sleep on the bed in his previous home. If you want to change this behaviour, start right away so that he learns what is expected of him. You will also have to decide how much

exercise to give. Some may have been given walks every day; others may have had little or no exercise. If your Stafford has been under-exercised, you will need to take it steady and gradually build up the amount he is given over a period of weeks. Generally an hour's exercise a day is sufficient to keep a Stafford in good condition, but you will need to tailor this to your dog's individual needs.

If the weather is very warm then avoid going out during the heat of the day. If possible walk early in the morning or later in the evening. Never exercise your Stafford after he has eaten; wait

for at least two hours before taking him out. You should also give a cooling down period at least an hour before feeding him following exercise.

Always walk your Stafford on the lead. You need to remember that he is an exuberant animal who is full of fun, and until he gets to know you, he is unlikely to respond to your every command. He needs to be taught to walk close to you and to sit or at least wait at the kerb. He also needs to be familiar with day-to-day distractions that he may not have encountered before, particularly if he is changing homes from town to country or vice versa.

Take time to get to know your Stafford and then you will know what care and exercise he requires.

There is no greater reward than seeing a rescued Staffordshire Bull Terrier settled in a new home.

If you are taking on a rescued Stafford with an existing dog, it is best to choose the opposite sex. Two bitches together may be okay, but never be tempted to have two males, as one will usually want to be top dog. It is always best to carry out the initial introduction on neutral territory, and most rescue workers will be prepared to meet with you and the other dog to establish whether they are likely to get along. If this goes well, the next step is to introduce the newcomer to your home. To begin with you will need to be vigilant, and do not allow them to be in each other's company without supervision for the first few weeks. A crate for one or both dogs may prove useful, as the dogs are safe in your absence but are still with each other. If you are careful over initial introductions, there is no reason why they should not become the best of friends.

Where cats are concerned, acceptance usually takes a little longer. Rescued Staffords who have previously lived in harmony with cats will not necessarily take to a new cat at first. A stairgate may help, as the animals are able to become familiar with each other, while the gate enables the cat to get out of the way, if necessary. With time and patience, most will eventually learn to accept one another and will at least tolerate each other.

It is extremely important to have patience with a rescued dog. Bear in mind that his past life may not have been easy, and he may have had a lot to contend with. It could also be that your Stafford comes from a home where he was greatly loved, and it may take him some time to come to terms with his new life. However, Staffords are very amiable and take most things in their stride. If treated kindly and fairly, he will repay you a thousandfold, making a loving and sociable family pet.

THE BEST OF CARE

Chapter 5

With his short coat and hardy constitution, the Stafford is considered to be a 'low maintenance' dog. However, in order to get the best from your Stafford and for him to lead a healthy and happy life, it is important to ensure that he has the best of care.

DIET AND NUTRITION

The underpinning for a healthy animal is, of course, the diet he is fed. This will give him a shiny coat, bright eyes, good weight, plenty of energy and the ability to fight off infections. One thing I have learnt over the many years that I have kept dogs is that there is no single diet that suits all dogs. Sometimes it is a matter of trial and error before you find the diet that is best for your dog and your lifestyle. In addition, you have to be prepared to adapt the

chosen diet to suit any altered conditions, such as old age, pregnancy or illness, which may affect your dog. Recently we had five dogs in the house and we were feeding three diets: two of the dogs were young and required a high-energy diet; two were elderly and required easily digestible, less energy packed food; and the fifth suffered from acute allergies, which were partly controlled by a special diet.

The energy requirements of a dog are the key to the diet choices. Energy here does not just mean the ability to run, jump and hunt, but also to lactate successfully, keep warm in cold conditions, and sustain bodyweight in stressful situations. In the last case, Staffords are one of the breeds renowned for losing weight in boarding kennels. All too often they find the situation stressful because they are away from the family, and, in spite of

eating their usual amount of food, they will still lose weight.

The dog is an omnivore and, as such, a meat-only diet is not suitable. There are a number of essential nutrients a dog requires:

Protein: A dog cannot survive without protein, so even if a dog is successfully reared on a vegetarian diet, it must contain protein and be supplemented by vitamin D. Proteins supply the 10 essential amino acids that all dogs need and which they cannot make on their own. Adult dogs normally need about 10 per cent of their total calories from protein.

Fats: Fats and fatty acids are another important element of a dog's diet, and these are obtained from animal fats or from the oils of plant seeds. Fats are the best source of energy for the dog, and fatty acids keep the dog's coat and skin healthy.

It is the energy requirements of a dog that should dictate his diet.

Carbohydrates: As well as protein and fats supplying the energy in a dog's diet, carbohydrates also play their part. These are usually supplied in the diet from cereal or plant foodstuffs.

Vitamins: These are essential to the health of a dog. Deficiency in vitamins can cause health problems. For example, a deficiency in vitamin D can cause rickets in a young animal.

Minerals: There are 12 minerals that are essential nutrients for the dog. They all have jobs to do in the body. For example, calcium and phosphorus are needed to produce strong bones and teeth. Deficiencies in these can cause problems, e.g. skeletal deformities, but on the other hand abnormalities can also occur when puppies are fed an excess of calcium.

There are detailed tables that stipulate the specific nutrients needed for the average dog of whatever weight/age. Calculating these tables takes a lot of time, and some mathematical accuracy. Fortunately, the choice of foods now available to the dog owner means that, for most of us, these calculations are not necessary since these foods have been the subject of trials and research by the food manufacturing companies.

TYPES OF DIET
Let us now look at the feeding methods available to us:

HOME-MADE DIET
You can feed your Stafford dog purely on 'home-made' food. Meat or other proteins can be obtained from many sources, and these can be mixed with commercially produced dog biscuit or even bread rusked (baked) in the oven. You should never use an all-in-one (complete) type food as a mixer. To be sure that your Stafford is getting all the correct elements of the diet, you will need to add supplements of vitamins, minerals etc., calculating that you are giving them in the correct quantities for your dog's good health.

BARF DIET
The BARF diet refers to Biologically Appropriate Raw Food (also known as Bones and Raw Food). It is a specialised form of home-feeding where only raw food is given. This includes meat, eggs and soft, uncooked

Supplements will need to be added to a home-made diet.

A complete diet is scientifically balanced to cater for all your dog's needs.

Canned food should be fed with a mixer.

bones (e.g. chicken wings, lambs necks etc.). Eggs, vegetables, whole raw fish and ground bone meal are also a part of this diet. It is essential to realise that cooked bones should never be given to a dog – whatever the diet you are following. Some commercial products, e.g. 'veggie burgers', are now available in the BARF diet regime. It would seem that additives (e.g. vitamins and probiotics) are often recommended by adherents of this form of feeding. Some people also recommend that foods are not combined in one meal, so it is suggested that meat is fed at one meal and carbohydrates at another. Vegetables can be served with either. Where bones are to be eaten raw, they should be soft. Hard bones (e.g. marrow or knuckle bones) are given separately as 'treats.'

As with any home-made diet, you will need to do a lot of research to make sure you are not depriving your dog of any important vitamins, minerals etc. On the other hand, you are giving the dog a diet that is close to what he would have if he were living in the wild.

COMMERCIAL FOOD

Commercial foods come in three types: dry, semi-moist and canned.

Dry food: The dry or complete foods come from cereal or animal sources. These can be served with water added. Clean water should always be available to dogs, but it is essential when you are feeding dried commercial foods that a ready supply is on hand. It is a temptation with this type of food to start giving the animal more than the stipulated amount, or to give additives. These foods have been developed following years of scientific research. All the elements necessary for the dog have been

balanced out. You should abide by the directions for the age/condition of your dog, as making additions upsets this balance.

Semi-moist food: This is usually sold in sachets; it is not as popular as the other two types of commercial food.

Canned: Both semi-moist and canned food should be fed with a carbohydrate addition (e.g. biscuit or mixer). Many commercial dog food producers make special mixers for use with their canned or semi-moist foods. Do not use the dried, complete food as a mixer with these other products or you will upset the balance. With canned meals, as with the other commercial products, all the elements needed by the dog are present. You should avoid making additions, as you can cause damage by exceeding a dog's requirements as surely as you can harm him with a deficiency.

An eight-week-old puppy's needs four small meals a day.

PUPPY DIET

Many breeders try to introduce their puppies to a variety of foods, including raw meat, eggs, cereal, and canned food. This could be of advantage to the new owner, who will probably want to give puppy the diet that they find easiest for their way of life.

When you collect your puppy you should receive a diet sheet, and it would be advisable to keep as closely as possible to this diet. If you do decide to change, it is important not to do a sudden, 'cold turkey' switch. Try to introduce the food you wish to give gradually. So you may take a week, for example, to get the puppy off his meat and biscuit diet and on to a full complete food diet.

Puppies do best with a number of small meals. We usually give four meals a day: two that are protein-based and two that are dairy-based (e.g. milk). As a pup grows, he will decide to cut down his meals quite naturally himself. Perhaps the first to go should be his last meal – this will help him to be clean in the night. Certainly the protein – usually meat – meals will take his fancy more than cereal and milk meals, so these can be gradually dropped. A Stafford puppy will be on two meals a day until he is at least nine months old. Remember: you gain nothing in the end by cutting down on a pup's food unless he is grossly overweight. Whatever you put into your Stafford as a youngster will pay you dividends when he is an adult.

ADULT DIET

An adult Stafford, who has a moderate amount of exercise, will only need one meal a day, and this can be fed morning or evening. Meals should not be fed immediately before violent exercise. It is estimated that an adult Stafford needs a daily intake of 30kcal per lb of bodyweight.

Whatever type of diet you finally decide to give your dog, there is only one that is not recommended and that is a human food. Feeding your dog the same food as you provide for yourself is the surest way to produce an overweight and unhealthy dog.

The older Stafford will not be as active as a young one. It will therefore be necessary to adapt his diet. We find that easily digestible – usually chicken- or tripe-based foods – suit the older dog best. The amounts could also be reduced and, in extreme circumstances, we prefer to feed the older dog two small meals – say, morning and evening – rather than one larger meal.

Meals should not be fed immediately before or after exercise.

OBESITY

The weight of dogs has been given a lot of publicity lately – generally where the dog is grossly overweight. Staffords seem to put on extra weight, as they grow older, probably because their exercise is reduced. Neutering also seems to increase the likelihood of an adult Stafford putting on extra pounds. Balancing diet and exercise is the key to maintaining good bodyweight.

Obesity diets are available commercially. A home-made remedy often used by show people is to feed a slightly smaller

SPECIAL DIETS

There are certain medical conditions that may require a special diet. Allergies are not uncommon in Staffords, and special diets are available for this. If you wish to try home-made remedies, salmon and mashed potatoes are the blandest diet to give. If you believe that food is causing the allergic reaction, try adding various foods to this basic recipe – one at a time – and see if there is any adverse reaction in your dog. In this way, you should be able to find exactly which food types activate the allergic reaction. Dogs suffering from other conditions, e.g. renal failure, will certainly need a diet recommended by your vet – again, there are commercial foods available for all these conditions.

A Staffordshire Bull Terrier should look lean and muscular, and carry no excess weight.

amount of food and add a little bran, or if you don't mind the flatulence, boiled cabbage. Both these additions fill the dog's stomach and make him 'feel' full up.

If a dog is overweight, it puts pressure on his heart, reduces his ability to exercise properly, puts strain on his joints, and the risk is increased if the dog needs a general anaesthetic. As a guideline, an ideal weight for a Stafford is when you can feel his ribs with your fingers; if you can't, then he is overweight.

SKINNY STAFFORDS

At present, it is quite fashionable to 'strip' Staffords out so that you can actually see the dog's ribs, and probably count his backbone into the bargain. Such a dog is too thin for normal living. Owners do not realise that keeping a dog – especially a Stafford – in this highly 'fit' condition also has an effect on him mentally. We know ourselves that if we greatly reduce our weight and increase our fitness routines, we can feel on a 'high'. Well, the same thing

PREGNANCY

In pregnancy, a Stafford bitch should be given the highest quality of food, but not in an increased amount. Only when she has had her puppies should you give her as much food as she can eat, without upsetting her bowels. The Stafford bitdh will need plenty of food to make sufficient milk of the best quality.

When a bitch is feeding puppies she requires maximum nutrition of the highest quality.

happens to a dog. People in welfare have actually told stories of managing to keep a Stafford in a home simply by recommending that the owners tackle the Stafford's extreme activity by adding a few pounds to his weight. Very often such animals slow down, relax and become much calmer and, quite simply, easier to live with.

FEEDING METHODS

There remains the actual method of giving the food. Some breeders rear puppies on the free-feeding method. This means that food is available all the time, and the puppies – and later the adults – eat at will. This is not a method that I have found very successful. I prefer to give puppies the amount necessary for their age,

and if they do not eat it all, I pick up what is left and they wait until the next meal. On the other hand, if the pups gobble it up and still look hungry, I make them a bit extra in the next meal.

Feeding adults together presents other problems. Some breeders believe that group feeding bonds the group as a family. With Staffords I have found that, in practice, one dog is the boss, and, if you are not careful, he will eat his own and everybody else's food as well. If anyone challenges this state of affairs, a fight can quickly ensue.

Recently, we had a pair of Staffords in for rehoming. The bitch of the pair was terrifyingly thin – so much so that we spent some of the welfare organisation's hard-earned money getting a vet to give her a check-up. We separated the pair in the kennels, so that they could go to two homes if necessary. After a week we noticed that the bitch, without any medical assistance, had put on weight. Enquiries told us that the two had been fed together unsupervised. Obviously the larger, more dominant, dog had been eating almost all of the bitch's food as well as his own!

So, from an early age, all our dogs have their own bowl. In this way we can vary the diet and the amounts of food to suit each animal. Sometimes we put the dogs in separate rooms to feed, but when they are in the same room they are kept well apart and are supervised. The bowls used for feeding a Stafford should, ideally, be stainless steel. A young Stafford can make short work of plastic bowls, and giving pottery or china bowls for water can be dangerous, as they can easily shatter.

FAST DAYS

Some breeders introduce a 'fasting' day into their feeding regime. Years ago it was common practice not to feed a dog on one day of the week – seeking, I suppose, to mimic the situation in the wild, where a dog might not be able to get a meal every day of the week.

Modern feeding methods are worked out on a seven-day feeding regime, so fasting is not often seen today. More commonly, breeders will add, no matter what feeding method they are using, an occasional tin of fatty fish, e.g. sardines. This is done in order to maximise the oils in the coat – nothing looks better than a Stafford's short coat gleaming in the sunshine.

If you have two Staffords, it is best to feed them separately so that they both get a fair share.

MEAL TIMES

The timing of meals is a matter of personal preference. We feed our dogs at the same time every day – in the evening. However, some breeders believe that you should vary the time, so the dog will not fret and worry as the time for his meal approaches.

Whatever time you feed your Stafford, make sure he is not fed just before you feed yourselves. It is now well documented that the order in which each member of a family eats establishes the 'pecking order' of that family. We avoid this problem by feeding the dogs at least an hour before we feed ourselves – so, everyone is happy!

Exercise should be strictly limited while a puppy is still growing.

EXERCISING YOUR STAFFORD

If you get the feeding right, you are more than halfway to owning a healthy, happy dog. But as we have seen, the type and amount of food we give a dog is a balancing act with the amount of exercise he gets. There are two reasons for exercising: fitness and mental happiness.

PUPPY EXERCISE

Stafford puppies do not need a great deal of walking before they are six months of age at least. Indeed, over-walking at an early age has been known to damage the pasterns and other joints. Pups should not be taken out until they have completed their course of injections. Then, the main purpose of taking pup out should be to get him used to walking on a collar and lead and introducing him to as many new experiences as possible. So, the best type of exercise for a young Stafford puppy is a short, educational walk along a busy road where he will hear lorries changing gear and meet people with pushchairs, children on bicycles, ladies with big bags of shopping, and maybe other dogs. I have known people take their young animals to a local market and just stand on the pavement, letting the pup soak up the atmosphere. (For more advice on socialisation, see Chapter Six.)

When your puppy is around six months of age, you can start more serious exercise: road walking and, hopefully, free running in wide, open spaces. There is no real substitute to a dog enjoying free exercise, following the smells, pushing through the undergrowth, splashing through the puddles… It may take longer to put muscle on a youngster if you exercise him in this way, but the mental benefits of free exercise far outweigh the ease of building muscle by forced exercise.

ADULT EXERCISE

A fully-grown, mature Stafford needs strenuous exercise. The easiest way of providing this is by simply throwing a ball, 10 to 20 times at a session. This also has the advantage of introducing a little bit of obedience, as you will need to train your Stafford to give the ball back to you so that you can throw it again.

We have to be socially aware when exercising our Staffords in public places such as parks. Always be prepared for the fact

EXERCISING YOUR STAFFORD

In Water

On Land

Playing Games

that some dog may come and challenge your Stafford. Make no mistake: if a fight ensues, no matter how much provocation your Stafford has had to endure, he will be branded the aggressor! It is therefore important to keep your dog under control at all times. If you know you have a 'naughty' dog, then use a stretch-type lead in public places. If your Stafford is very intent on his ball game, he may well ignore all the other dogs in the park – providing they don't try to get his ball!

While you may have to avoid confrontation with other dogs when you have an adult Stafford, it is just as important to protect your pup when he is too young

to defend himself. Don't let a bigger dog do him harm when he is young, as he will never forget the trauma. When he is grown up, you may well find that he is aggressive towards any dog that reminds him of this original tormentor.

Walking with a single Stafford, who is in harmony with you, is one of the greatest pleasures you will get from a dog. In general, Staffords do not need miles and miles of exercise. They will certainly love a long ramble, but can be kept fit and happy with much less than a 10-mile hike, and that is why they adapt equally well to town life and country life.

PLAYING GAMES

There has never been more variety of toys available to dog owners than there is today. Staffords are fun-loving dogs and enjoy a good game. Personally, I like to play games with dogs where I have the upper hand. Therefore, I don't go in for wrestling games; a Stafford is too strong and doesn't always know his own strength. If you keep more than one Stafford, they can play wrestling with each other!

Games of hide-and-seek are great fun for dog and human. Your Stafford can be encouraged to look for objects, and you can make a big fuss of him when he finds the hidden object. We sold a Stafford to a lady who played energetic games of 'find the piece of cheese', which involved searching under and over every piece of furniture in her living room. Children love this game, and they can even go and hide, and wait to be found by the Stafford. I know of one little boy who thought of the most intriguing places to hide – from the obvious ducking down behind the settee to wrapping himself in the long window curtains. Eventually, the bitch always found him. This game built up a wonderful rapport between dog and child, and was far more rewarding for the two of them than the expensive toys on offer.

Pulling toys are popular with Staffords, but be careful with an immature youngster where their teeth may not yet be fixed in the gums. Where you have more than one Stafford, care should be taken not to over-excite them with games, as this can end in major fall-outs. At the end of the day the ball or Frisbee type of toy, where the dog can run and retrieve, are still the most popular. Remember that the ball must be very hard for a Stafford; it should not be so small that it could jam down his throat, nor so large as to be difficult for his jaws to accommodate.

Footballs are great fun for the Stafford, but unfortunately they do not last very long, as they

TAKE A DIP

Hydro pools are becoming a popular method of exercising dogs. Such a form of exercise is extremely good for an animal recovering from an injury or from an operation, as it provides exercise without putting stress on the dog's joints. I don't see it as a substitute for a proper walk, but as an excellent addition or alternative in special circumstances.

puncture too easily. Pointed sticks are dangerous for any dog to chase. If they point into the ground as they fall, a dog can jam the stick through the roof of his mouth. Stones are another 'no no', as they break and discolour teeth.

If you are doing obedience with your dog, training him for the show ring or even just introducing him to basic commands, always start your lessons after he has had a chance to release his energies by a good walk or an energetic activity. (For information on training, see Chapter Six.)

GROOMING YOUR STAFFORD

The basics for a healthy dog are food and exercise. But even with a short-coated dog such as the Stafford, grooming will enhance his looks and improve his physical well-being.

All Staffords moult during the

year, and especially in warm weather. So a good grooming with a hard bristle brush will help reduce the loose hairs and encourage a close, shiny coat, which is so desirable in the breed. Some Staffords, blacks and black brindles in particular, may have long hairs in their coat, so more grooming may be necessary. You can use a bristle brush, but most Stafford owners prefer to use a rubber mitt, which removes dead hairs and brings out the shine in the coat. While you are giving your Stafford a brush to remove dead hairs, it is a good idea to take a look at other parts of him so you can spot any problems at an early stage.

EYES

Your Stafford's eyes should be clear and bright, and should not water a lot. If you see severe watering, you should consult your vet just in case there is a problem, such as extra or in-growing lashes.

EARS

Your Stafford may suffer from ear mites or similar problems. It would appear that some Staffords have very narrow ear canals, which exacerbate the problems. In bad cases, the dog will shake his head and scratch his ears. When you check the ears, you should also smell them; a mousy aroma is often the first tell-tale sign of an

GROOMING YOUR STAFFORD

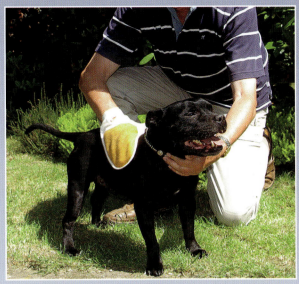

A rubber mitt helps to remove dead hairs and brings out the shine in the coat.

Teeth should be checked and cleaned when necessary.

You may find it easier to recruit an assistant to help with nail trimming.

The tail is scissored from underneath to give a whip-like appearance.

infected ear. Consult your vet if your Stafford is experiencing ear problems – and never, never, dig down into the ear canal.

TEETH

Your Stafford should get used to having his mouth examined from an early age. When he is changing from milk teeth to adult teeth, at around four months of age, his mouth will be rather tender, so be especially careful at this time. You should look to see that he is losing his teeth correctly – that is, that the second teeth come up and push out the baby (milk) teeth.

Occasionally Staffords retain the first teeth, especially the canines. Such retention can cause problems when two sets of teeth are in situ. You can gently wiggle the baby teeth or give the pup something to chew that will bring out the first set of teeth. If you are concerned about your Stafford's teeth, consult your vet.

As the dog grows older, you will need to check that there is no discolouration or tooth decay. There are a few ways for you to keep your Stafford's teeth clean. You can buy special chews for this purpose. Alternatively, you can clean his teeth; a normal toothbrush can be used, and there are special dog toothpastes available, which are suitably flavoured with beef or lamb, etc.

BONE OF CONTENTION

Giving bones to keep your dog's teeth clean is a source of some disagreement. I find vets are particularly alarmed, as they see so many dogs with problems caused by bones. However, giving a large marrow or knuckle bone is the best treat you can give your dog. The bone must be large and raw, as a cooked bone can splinter (and the Stafford has very strong jaws, remember).

Bones are the easiest way to get otherwise friendly dogs falling out with one another, so be very careful. You may also find that your Stafford takes the bone and merely buries it. Don't be fooled into thinking he doesn't fancy the bone; some weeks later he will surely dig it up again. By then it is smelly, but seemingly even more attractive to the dog.

In my opinion, if sufficient care is taken, providing bones is a very good and natural way for a dog to keep his teeth clean.

FEET AND NAILS

If the Stafford has a well-constructed foot – that is, a shape halfway between the cat and the hare – and with plenty of depth or cushioning to the pad, then he will naturally keep his nails short. If, however, the dog has a hare foot with long toes, then the nails may easily grow long and cause problems. Extra work on pavements or other hard surfaces may help. Otherwise, it will be necessary to file or cut the nails.

Large metal files can be used, and there are now some excellent dog clippers on the market. Your puppy should have had his nails cut several times before you collect him. It will be to your advantage if you continue to handle his feet. Even if you don't need to cut his nails, get him used to having his feet picked up and having his nails examined. If you put slight pressure on the knuckles of the toes, the nail will protrude and you will see more easily where the blood vessels enter the nail. If you need to cut the nails, your Stafford will not resent being handled in this way. Be careful not to cut into the quick of the nail or it will bleed quite profusely.

The pads should cause little trouble, unless you walk your Stafford on hot tarmac in the summer, or on salted surfaces in the winter. In both cases, blisters may result.

BATH TIME

Staffords should rarely be bathed. When it is necessary, most Staffords will tolerate the procedure, even if they don't like it. I find that using a shower is the easiest method. If the shower base is plastic, you will need to line it with towels or a rubber mat to provide a non-slip surface.

Make sure the water is not too hot, and use dog shampoo. Be careful to protect the eyes from the shampoo, and hold down the ears, as you do not want water seeping into them. Massage the shampoo into a good foam, and make sure you cover all parts of the dog. Use plenty of warm, clean water to rinse the coat – this is the big advantage of using a shower.

Once your Stafford emerges from the shower cubicle, hold a towel like an umbrella over the top of him and allow him to give himself a really good shake. Then towel him down to dry the coat. You will not need to use a hair-dryer on the short-coated Stafford.

We are lucky that Staffords need minimal work to be exhibited in the show ring.

SHOW PRESENTATION

If you plan to show your Stafford, give him a bath a couple of days before the show. Bathing sometimes brings up dandruff on the dog's coat, which is unsightly in the show ring. When he is dry, hand massage him to bring up the natural oils in his coat.

A Stafford with a lot of white on his coat may look dirty, but it is better to wash the white bits rather than giving a full bath too often, as bathing can easily strip the oils in a dog's coat. Chalking a white dog is a good way to clean him, but remember, residual chalk is not allowed under Kennel Club rules, in the show ring.

Tonsuring (i.e. trimming with scissors or clippers) is almost unknown in the Stafford with the exception of the tail, which is almost always scissored underneath in order to give a whip-like appearance. Alternatively, a good appearance can be obtained by using a beard razor on the tail. Scissoring is allowed in the UK, although not in some other countries. For example, in the USA, the American Kennel Club Breed Standard states: "Coat, smooth, short and close to the skin. Not to be trimmed or de-whiskered". Years ago people used to cut the whiskers off Staffords in order to make the muzzle look extremely 'clean'. Thankfully, this procedure is hardly ever followed in the UK today.

VETERINARY CARE

A very serious part of caring for your Stafford is to keep abreast with the latest veterinary procedures on offer. Make sure you keep his injections against the well-known doggy diseases up to date. If you need to leave your Stafford while you go away, proof of inoculation will be required by boarding kennels. Staffords can be escape artists, and while you may think that you are being 'kind' to leave your dog with a neighbour, unless that person understands the Stafford you could return to a disaster. Many kennels will also require a kennel cough inoculation.

Routine worming, with a product recommended by your vet, is an absolute necessity. We all know the dangers of disease affecting children as a result of worms in the faeces. So make a note on your calendar to remind you to worm your Stafford. If you notice him rubbing his bottom on the ground, think first of worms. If that fails to cure the problem, then a blocked anal gland could be the cause, and you will need to consult your vet.

While you are doing the routine brushing, you might also look out for signs of fleas or ticks. There are excellent products on the market to rid your dog of these. Remember that fleas will also inhabit your house and the dog's bed, and if you have a cat or hedgehogs in the garden, the dog can quickly re-infest himself.

Should you decide to breed your Stafford, make sure you have had his/her eyes tested, and that you have the DNA tests for hereditary cataracts and L-2 Hydroxyglutaricacid uria (L-2HGA), or have proof that he/she is hereditarily clear of these conditions.

Being rather headstrong and so full of life, Staffords tend to be accident-prone. It is therefore necessary for any caring owner to be aware of possible dangers at all times. Be wary of ever saying, "He will never jump out of the car, the window, over that fence, go through the front door…" Staffords are renowned for proving the unexpected. It is strongly recommended that you take out insurance on your pet.

There remains one last condition for the optimum care of your Stafford and that is quite simply that you ensure he has plenty of human companionship and 'quality time'. Above all, the Stafford is a family dog – all his other activities are secondary to this. He is an extremely sociable animal – at least with anything on two legs, if not on four. The worst punishment you can inflict on a Stafford is to ignore him. Spending hours on his own in a kennel or a crate is not giving a Stafford the best of care. Only living in the house with his family – especially children – do you see the very best of this wonderful breed.

Staffordshire Bull Terriers have a tendency to be headstrong, so accidents can happen.

With luck, your Stafford will live to a ripe old age, enjoying life to the full.

SAYING GOODBYE

The average Stafford will live until ten or twelve years of age. Many live longer and some, mainly from accidental causes will have shorter lives. As they grow older they will, of course, develop problems – hearing loss and arthritis being the most common. Today there are a number of remedies on the market to alleviate many of the problems. However, as time goes by, caring owners may well have to ask themselves the uncomfortable question – how good is the quality of life for this dog? We have to be brutally honest with ourselves, as it could be that we are prolonging his life more for our comfort than his enjoyment. Unlike humans, we cannot amuse them with the television, books or music. Losing normal functions – walking or running – is more of a loss to an animal than to a human. A normally clean Stafford can be extremely distressed if he becomes incontinent. Staffords have a high pain threshold but that does not mean that they do not experience pain at all.

At the end, the most caring thing we might be asked to do for our pet is to agree a peaceful, painless euthanasia.

You could ask your vet to do a home visit if you have a dog that is distressed by visiting the vet. But wherever you are, I would urge you to stay with your dog until the end. You really will feel better in yourself if you have been able to speak to and comfort him right until he closes his eyes. You will probably not realise at first that he has 'gone'. Do not be afraid of your grief – this is so common even among those of us who have owned many, many dogs. Each one is an individual and with their passing another chapter of our lives closes and it is natural to mourn their loss.

TRAINING AND SOCIALISATION

Chapter 6

When you decided to bring a Staffordshire Bull Terrier into your life, you probably had dreams of how it was going to be: energetic walks and play sessions, cosy evenings with a Stafford lying devotedly at your feet, and an enthusiastic welcome whenever you returned home.

There is no doubt that you can achieve all this – and much more – with a Stafford, but like anything that is worth having, you must be prepared to put in the work. A Stafford, regardless of whether it is a puppy or an adult, does not come ready trained, understanding exactly what you want and fitting perfectly into your lifestyle. A Stafford has to learn his place in your family and he must discover what is acceptable behaviour.

We have a great starting point in that the Staffordshire Bull Terrier has an outstanding temperament. This is a dog who loves his family, and wants nothing more than to be in the hub of all activities. He is known for his reliable temperament, and a well-trained Stafford is a joy to own. However, responsible owners must be aware of the Stafford's ancestry.

The breed was developed as a fighting dog, and although dog fighting has been banned for over 150 years, instincts can run very deep. The best Stafford breeders will only use dogs of exemplary character in order that the breed's best traits are strengthened and reproduced. But it would be unwise to take on a Stafford without considering that he may have problems with other dogs. Staffords can live peaceably together, but this is not always the case. Owners need to be dog savvy, and be aware of potential areas of conflict, both with dogs living at home, and dogs in public places.

THE FAMILY PACK

Dogs have been domesticated for some 14,000 years, but, luckily for us, they have inherited and retained behaviour from their distant ancestor – the wolf. A Staffordshire Bull Terrier may never have lived in the wild, but he is born with the survival skills and the mentality of a meat-eating predator who hunts in a pack. A wolf living in a pack owes its existence to mutual co-operation and an acceptance of a hierarchy, as this ensures both food and protection. A domesticated dog living in a family pack has exactly the same outlook. He wants food, companionship, and leadership – and it is your job to provide for these needs.

YOUR ROLE

Theories about dog behaviour and methods of training go in and out of fashion, but in reality, nothing has changed from the day when wolves ventured in from the wild to join the family circle. The wolf (and equally the dog) accepts a subservient place in the family pack in return for food and protection. In a dog's eyes you are his leader, and he relies on you to make all the important decisions. This does not mean that you have to act like a dictator or a bully. You are accepted as a leader, without argument, as long as you have the right credentials.

The first part of the job is easy. You are the provider, and you are therefore respected because you supply food. In a Stafford's eyes, you must be the ultimate hunter because a day never goes by when you cannot find food. The second part of the leader's job description is straightforward, but for some reason we find it hard to achieve. In order for a dog to accept his place in the family pack he must respect his leader as the decision-maker. A low-ranking pack animal does not question authority; he is perfectly happy to see someone else shoulder the responsibility. Problems will only arise if you cut a poor figure as leader and the dog feels he should mount a challenge for the top-ranking role.

Can you be a firm, fair and consistent leader?

The Stafford is quick to learn both good and bad habits.

HOW TO BE A GOOD LEADER

There are a number of guidelines to follow to establish yourself in the role of leader in a way that your Stafford understands and respects. If you have a puppy, you may think you don't have to take this on board for a few months, but that would be a big mistake. Start as you mean to go on, and your pup will be quick to find his place in his new family.

- **Keep it simple:** Decide on the rules you want your Stafford to obey and always make it 100 per cent clear what is acceptable, and what is unacceptable, behaviour.

- **Be consistent:** If you are not consistent about enforcing rules, how can you expect your Stafford to take you seriously? There is nothing worse than allowing your Stafford to jump up at you one moment and then scolding him the next time he does it because you were wearing your best clothes. As far as the Stafford is concerned, he may as well try it on because he can't predict your reaction.

- **Get your timing right:** If you are rewarding your Stafford or, and equally if you are reprimanding him, you must respond within one to two seconds otherwise the dog will not link his behaviour with your reaction (see page 88).

- **Read your dog's body language:** Find out how to read body language and facial expressions (see page 86) so that you understand your Stafford's feelings and his intentions.

- **Be aware of your own body language:** When you ask your Stafford to do something, do not bend over him and talk to him at eye level. Assert your authority by standing over him and keeping an upright posture. You can also help your dog to learn by using your body language to communicate with him. For example, if you want your dog to come to you, open your arms out and look inviting. If you want your dog to stay, use a hand signal (palm flat, facing the dog) so you are effectively 'blocking' his advance.

- **Tone of voice:** Dogs are very receptive to tone of voice, so you can use your voice to praise him or to correct undesirable behaviour. If you are pleased with your Stafford, praise him to the skies in a warm, happy voice. If you want to stop him raiding the bin, use a deep, stern voice when you say "No".

- **Give one command only:** If you keep repeating a command, or keep changing it, your Stafford will think you are babbling and will probably ignore you. If your Stafford does not respond the first time you ask, make it simple by using a treat to lure him into position, and then you can reward him for a correct response.

- **Daily reminders:** A young, exuberant Stafford is apt to forget his manners from time to time, and an adolescent dog may attempt to challenge your

85

authority (see page 98). Rather than coming down on your Stafford like a ton of bricks when he does something wrong, try to prevent bad manners by daily reminders of good manners. For example:

i Do not let your dog barge ahead of you when you are going through a door.

ii Do not let him leap out of the car the moment you open the door (which could be potentially lethal, as well as being disrespectful).

iii Do not let him eat from your hand when you are at the table.

iv Do not let him 'win' a toy at the end of a play session and then make off with it. You 'own' his toys, and you must end every play session on your terms.

UNDERSTANDING YOUR STAFFORD

Body language is an important means of communication between dogs, which they use to make friends, to assert status, and to avoid conflict. It is important to get on your dog's wavelength by understanding his body language and reading his facial expressions.

- A positive body posture and a wagging tail indicate a happy, confident dog.
- A crouched body posture with ears back and tail down show that a dog is being submissive. A dog may do this when he is being told off or if a more assertive dog approaches him.
- A bold dog will stand tall, looking strong and alert. His ears will be forward and his tail will be held high.
- A dog who raises his hackles (lifting the fur along his topline) is trying to look as scary as possible. This may be the prelude to aggressive behaviour, but, in many cases, the dog is apprehensive and is unsure how to cope with a situation.
- A playful dog will go down on his front legs while standing on his hind legs in a bow position. This friendly invitation says: "I'm no threat, let's play."
- A dominant, aggressive dog will meet other dogs with a hard stare. If he is challenged, he may bare his teeth and growl, and the corners of his mouth will be drawn forward. His ears will be forward and he will appear tense in every muscle (see page 102).

If you learn to read your Stafford's body language, you will understand his intentions.

- A nervous dog will often show aggressive behaviour as a means of self-protection. If threatened, this dog will lower his head and flatten his ears. The corners of his mouth may be drawn back, and he may bark or whine.
- The Stafford is king of meeting and greeting. A friendly Stafford will almost tie himself in knots when he is meeting human friends and family. Do not mistake whines and rumblings as being sinister. The Stafford is a great 'talker' and will express his pleasure vocally.

GIVING REWARDS

Why should your Stafford do as you ask? If you follow the guidelines given above, your Stafford should respect your authority, but what about the time when he has found a really enticing scent? The answer is that you must always be the most interesting, the most attractive, and the most irresistible person in your Stafford's eyes. It would be nice to think you could achieve this by personality alone, but most of us need a little extra help. You need to find out what is the biggest reward for your dog. In a Stafford's case, this could be a food treat or a toy. Some Staffords are real foodies, and will do anything for a tasty morsel, while others are motivated by toys, and the biggest reward is a play session with a favourite toy. Whatever reward you use, it must be something that your dog really wants.

Reward your Stafford when you get his attention so that he thinks it is fun to be with you.

TOP TREATS

Some trainers grade treats depending on what they are asking the dog to do. A dog may get a low-grade treat, such as a piece of dry food, to reward good behaviour on a random basis, such as sitting when you open a door or allowing you to examine his teeth. But high-grade treats, which may be cooked liver, sausage or cheese, are reserved for training new exercises or for use in the park when you want a really good recall. Whatever type of treat you use, remember to subtract it from your Stafford's daily ration. Fat Staffords are lethargic, prone to health problems, and will almost certainly have a shorter life expectancy. Reward your Stafford, but always keep a check on his figure!

When you are teaching a dog a new exercise, you should reward him frequently. When he knows the exercise or command, reward him randomly so that he keeps on responding to you in a positive manner. If your dog does something extra special, like leaving his canine chum mid-play in the park, make sure he really knows how pleased you are by giving him a handful of treats or throwing his ball a few extra times. If he gets a bonanza reward, he is more likely to come back on future occasions, because you have proved to be even more rewarding than his previous activity.

HOW DO DOGS LEARN?

It is not difficult to get inside your Stafford's head and understand how he learns, as it is not dissimilar to the way we learn. Dogs learn by conditioning: they find out that specific behaviours produce specific consequences. This is known as operant conditioning or consequence learning. Consequences have to be immediate or clearly linked to the behaviour, as a dog sees the world in terms of action and result. Dogs will quickly learn if an action has a bad consequence or a good consequence.

Dogs also learn by association.

This is known as classical conditioning or association learning. It is the type of learning made famous by Pavlov's experiment with dogs. Pavlov presented dogs with food and measured their salivary response (how much they drooled). Then he rang a bell just before presenting the food. At first, the dogs did not salivate until the food was presented. But after a while they learnt that the sound of the bell meant that food was coming, and so they salivated when they heard the bell. A dog needs to learn the association in order for it to have any meaning. For example, a dog that has never

THE CLICKER REVOLUTION

Karen Pryor pioneered the technique of clicker training when she was working with dolphins. It is very much a continuation of Pavlov's work and makes full use of association learning.

Karen wanted to mark 'correct' behaviour at the precise moment it happened. She found it was impossible to toss a fish to a dolphin when it was in mid-air, when she wanted to reward it. Her aim was to establish a conditioned response so the dolphin knew that it had performed correctly and a reward would follow.

The solution was the clicker: a small matchbox-shaped training aid, with a metal tongue that makes a click when it is pressed. To begin with, the dolphin had to learn that a click meant that food was coming. The dolphin then learnt that it

must 'earn' a click in order to get a reward. Clicker training has been used with many different animals, most particularly with dogs, and it has proved hugely successful. It is a great aid for pet owners and is also widely used by professional trainers who teach highly specialised skills.

seen a lead before will be completely indifferent to it. A dog that has learnt that a lead means he is going for a walk will get excited the second he sees the lead; he has learnt to associate a lead with a walk.

BE POSITIVE

The most effective method of training dogs is to use their ability to learn by consequence and to teach that the behaviour you want produces a good consequence. For example, if you ask your Stafford to "Sit", and reward him with a treat, he will learn that it is worth his while to sit on command because it will lead to a treat. He is far more likely to repeat the behaviour, and the behaviour will become stronger, because it results in a positive outcome. This method of training is known as positive reinforcement, and it generally leads to a happy, co-operative dog that is willing to work, and a handler who has fun training their dog.

The opposite approach is negative reinforcement. This is far less effective and often results in a poor relationship between dog and owner. In this method of training, you ask your Stafford to "Sit", and, if he does not respond, you deliver a sharp yank on the training collar or push his rear to the ground. The dog learns that not responding to your command has a bad consequence, and he may be less likely to ignore you in the future. However, it may well have a bad consequence for you, too. A dog

A puppy has a limited concentration span, so keep training sessions short, always ending on a positive note.

that is treated in this way may associate harsh handling with the handler and become aggressive or fearful. Instead of establishing a pattern of willing co-operation, you are establishing a relationship built on coercion.

GETTING STARTED

As you train your Stafford, you will develop your own techniques as you get to know what motivates him. You may decide to get involved with clicker training or you may prefer to go for a simple command-and-reward

formula. It does not matter what form of training you use, as long as it is based on positive, reward-based methods.

There are a few important guidelines to bear in mind when you are training your Stafford:

- Find a training area that is free from distractions, particularly when you are just starting out.
- Keep training sessions short, especially with young puppies that have very short attention spans.
- Do not train if you are in a bad

mood or if you are on a tight schedule – the training session will be doomed to failure.

- If you are using a toy as a reward, make sure it is only available when you are training. In this way it has an added value for your Stafford.
- If you are using food treats, make sure they are bite-size and easy to swallow; you don't want to hang about while your Stafford chews on his treat.
- All food treats must be deducted from your Stafford's daily food ration.
- When you are training, move around your allocated area so that your dog does not think that an exercise can only be performed in one place.
- If your Stafford is finding an exercise difficult, try not to get frustrated. Go back a step and praise him for his effort. You will probably find he is more successful when you try again at the next training session.
- Always end training sessions on a happy, positive note. Ask your Stafford to do something you know he can do – it could be a trick he enjoys performing – and then reward him with a few treats or an extra-long play session.

In the exercises that follow, clicker training is introduced and followed, but all the exercises will work without the use of a clicker.

Use a treat to lure your Stafford into the Sit.

INTRODUCING A CLICKER

This is dead easy, and the intelligent Stafford will learn about the clicker in record time! It can be combined with attention training, which is a very useful tool and can be used on many different occasions.

- Prepare some treats and go to an area that is free from distractions. When your Stafford stops sniffing around and looks at you, click and reward by throwing him a treat. This means he will not crowd you, but will go looking for the treat. Repeat a couple of times. If your Stafford is very easily distracted, you may need to start this exercise with the dog on a lead.
- After a few clicks, your Stafford understands that if he hears a click, he will get a treat. He must now learn that he must 'earn' a click. This time, when your Stafford looks at you, wait a little longer before clicking, and then reward him. If your Stafford is on a lead but responding well, try him off the lead.
- When your Stafford is working for a click and giving you his attention, you can introduce a cue or command word, such as "Watch". Repeat a few times, using the cue. You now have a Stafford that understands the clicker and will give you his attention when you ask him to "Watch".

Lower a treat to the ground, and your Stafford will follow it until he goes into the Down position.

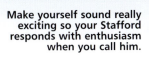

Make yourself sound really exciting so your Stafford responds with enthusiasm when you call him.

TRAINING EXERCISES

THE SIT
This is the easiest exercise to teach, so it is rewarding for both you and your Stafford.

- Choose a tasty treat and hold it just above your puppy's nose. As he looks up at the treat, he will naturally go into the Sit. As soon as he is in position, reward him.
- Repeat the exercise, and when your pup understands what you want, introduce the "Sit" command.
- If your Stafford is working for a toy, it is just as easy to lure him into position, and then reward him with a brief play session.

THE DOWN
Work hard at this exercise because a reliable Down is useful in many different situations, and an instant Down can be a lifesaver.

- You can start with your dog in a Sit, or it is just as effective to teach it when the dog is standing. Hold a treat just below your puppy's nose, and slowly lower it towards the ground. The treat acts as a lure, and your puppy will follow it, first going down on this forequarters, and then bringing his hindquarters down as he tries to get the treat.
- Make sure you close your fist around the treat, and only reward your puppy with the

treat when he is in the correct position. If your puppy is reluctant to go Down, you can apply gentle pressure on his shoulders to encourage him to go into the correct position.
- When your puppy is following the treat and going in to position, introduce a verbal command.
- Build up this exercise over a period of time, each time waiting a little longer before giving the reward, so the puppy learns to stay in the Down position.

THE RECALL
It is never too soon to start training the Recall. In fact, if you have a puppy it is best to start almost from the moment the

puppy arrives home, as he has a strong instinct to follow you. In most cases, a Stafford is only too keen to return to his owner, and you will find that he will match the enthusiasm you put into the exercise. Make yourself sound happy and excited, and your Stafford will come hurtling towards you!

- You can start teaching the Recall from the moment your puppy arrives home. He will naturally follow you, so keep calling his name, and reward him each time he comes to you.
- Practise in the garden, and, when your puppy is busy exploring, get his attention by calling his name. As he runs towards you, introduce the verbal command "Come". Make sure you sound happy and exciting, so your puppy wants to come to you. When he responds, give him lots of praise.
- If your puppy is slow to respond, try running away a few paces, or jumping up and down. It doesn't matter how silly you look, the key issue is to get your puppy's attention, and then make yourself irresistible!
- In a dog's mind, coming when called should be regarded as the best fun because he knows he is always going to be rewarded.

Never make the mistake of telling your dog off, no matter how slow he is to respond, as you will undo all your previous hard work.

- When you are free running your dog, make sure you have his favourite toy, or a pocket full of treats so you can reward him at intervals throughout the walk when you call him to you. Do not allow your dog to free run and only call him back at the end of the walk to clip his lead on. An intelligent Stafford will soon realise that the Recall means the end of his walk, and then the end of fun – so who can blame him for not wanting to come back?

SECRET WEAPON

You can build up a strong Recall by using another form of association learning. Buy a whistle, and when you are giving your Stafford his food, peep on the whistle. You can choose the type of signal you want to give: two short peeps or one long whistle, for example. Within a matter of days, your dog will learn that the sound of the whistle means that food is coming.

Now transfer the lesson outside. Arm yourself with some tasty treats and the whistle. Allow your Stafford to run free in the garden, and, after a couple of minutes, use the whistle. The dog has already learnt to associate the whistle with food, so he will come towards you. Immediately reward him with a treat and lots of praise. Repeat the lesson a few times in the garden so you are confident that your dog is responding before trying it in the park. Make sure you always have some treats in your pocket when you go for a walk, and your dog will quickly learn how rewarding it is to come to you.

TRAINING LINE

This is the equivalent of a very long lead, which you can buy at a pet store, or you can make your own with a length of rope. The training line is attached to your Stafford's collar and should be around 15 feet (4.5 metres) in length.

The purpose of the training line is to prevent your Stafford from disobeying you so that he never has the chance to get into bad habits. For example, when you call your Stafford and he ignores you, you can immediately pick up the end of the training line and call him again. By picking up the line you will have attracted his attention, and if you call him in an excited, happy voice, your Stafford will come to you. The moment he comes to you, give him a tasty treat so he is instantly rewarded for making the 'right' decision.

The training line is very useful when your Stafford becomes an adolescent and is testing your leadership. When you have reinforced the correct behaviour a number of times, your dog will build up a strong recall and you will not need to use a training line.

WALKING ON A LOOSE LEAD

This is a simple exercise, which baffles many Stafford owners. In most cases, owners are too impatient, wanting to get on with the expedition rather that training the dog how to walk on a lead. Take time with this one; the Stafford is a strong dog, and a Stafford that pulls on the lead is

With practice, your Stafford will learn to walk on a loose lead.

no pleasure to own. Many Stafford owners report that their dogs seem to have no traffic sense. For this reason, it is essential to keep your dog on a lead in built-up areas, and to train him to walk calmly by your side.

- In the early stages of lead training, allow your puppy to pick his route and follow him. He will get used to feeling 'attached' to you, and has no

reason to put up any resistance.
- Next, find a toy or a tasty treat and show it to your puppy. Let him follow the treat/toy for a few paces, and then reward him.
- Build up the amount of time your pup will walk with you, and when he is walking nicely by your side, introduce the verbal command" Heel" or "Close". Give lots of praise when your pup is in the correct position.

Teach your Stafford to "Stay" in easy stages.

Stafford to stay in position, even if it is only for a few seconds. The classic example is when you want your Stafford to stay in the back of the car until you have clipped on his lead.

Some trainers use the verbal command "Stay" when the dog is to stay in position for an extended period of time, and "Wait" if the dog is to stay in position for a few seconds until you give the next command. Others trainers use a universal "Stay" to cover all situations. It all comes down to personal preference, and as long as you are consistent, your dog will understand the command he is given.

- Put your puppy in a Sit or a Down, and use a hand signal (flat palm, facing the dog) to show he is to stay in position. Step a pace away from the dog. Wait a second, step back and reward him. If you have a lively pup, you may find it easier to train this exercise on the lead.
- Repeat the exercise, gradually increasing the distance you can leave your dog. When you return to your dog's side, praise him quietly, and release him with a command, such as "OK".
- Remember to keep your body language very still when you are training this exercise, and avoid eye contact with your dog. Work on this exercise over a period of time, and you will build up a really reliable Stay.

- When your pup is walking alongside you, keep focusing his attention on you by using his name, and then rewarding him when he looks at you. If it is going well, introduce some changes of direction.
- Do not attempt to take your puppy out on the lead, until you have mastered the basics at home. You need to be confident that your puppy accepts the lead and will focus his attention on you, when requested, before you face the challenge of a busy environment.
- As your Stafford gets bigger and stronger, he may try to pull on the lead, particularly if you are heading somewhere he wants to go, such as the park. If this happens, stop, call your dog to you, and do not set off again until he is in the correct position. It may take time, but your Stafford will eventually realise that it is more productive to walk by your side than to pull ahead.

STAYS

This may not be the most exciting exercise, but it is one of the most useful. There are many occasions when you want your

Take your Stafford out and about as soon as he has completed his course of vaccinations, giving him the opportunity to experience different situations.

SOCIALISATION

While your Stafford is mastering basic obedience exercises, there is other, equally important, work to do with him. A Stafford is not only becoming a part of your home and family, he is becoming a member of the community. He needs to be able to live in the outside world, coping calmly with every new situation that comes his way. It is your job to introduce him to as many different experiences as possible, and encourage him to behave in an appropriate manner. Socialisation is essential with all dogs, but with a Stafford it is of paramount importance. If you introduce your Stafford to other dogs and livestock at an early age, and curb any sign of aggression, you will encourage him to show the most amiable side of his disposition.

In order to socialise your Stafford effectively, it is helpful to understand how his brain is developing, and then you will get a perspective on how he sees the world.

CANINE SOCIALISATION (Birth to 7 weeks)

This is the time when a dog learns how to be a dog. By interacting with his mother and his littermates, a young pup learns about leadership and submission. He learns to read body posture so that he understands the intentions of his mother and his siblings. A puppy that is taken away from his litter too early may always have behavioural problems with other dogs, either being fearful or aggressive.

SOCIALISATION PERIOD (7 to 12 weeks)

This is the time to get cracking and introduce your Stafford puppy to as many different experiences as possible. This includes meeting different people, other dogs and animals, seeing new sights, and hearing a range of sounds, from the vacuum cleaner to the roar of traffic. At this stage, a puppy learns very quickly and what he learns will stay with him for the

A well-trained Stafford is a pleasure to take out.

firework going off, but you cannot always protect your puppy from the unexpected. If your pup has a nasty experience, the best plan is to make light of it and distract him by offering him a treat or a game. The pup will take the lead from you and will be reassured that there is nothing to worry about. If you mollycoddle him and sympathise with him, he is far more likely to retain the memory of his fear.

SENIORITY PERIOD (12 to 16 weeks)

During this period, your Stafford puppy starts to cut the apron strings and becomes more independent. He will test out his status to find out who is the pack leader: him or you. Bad habits, such as play biting, which may have been seen as endearing a few weeks earlier, should be firmly discouraged. Remember to use positive, reward-based training, but make sure your puppy knows that you are the leader and must be respected.

SECOND FEAR-IMPRINT PERIOD (6 to 14 months)

This period is not as critical as the first fear-imprint period, but it should still be handled carefully. During this time your Stafford may appear apprehensive, or he may show fear of something familiar. You may feel as if you have taken a backwards step, but if you adopt a calm, positive manner, your Stafford will see that there is nothing to be frightened of. Do

rest of his life. This is the best time for a puppy to move to a new home, as he is adaptable and ready to form deep bonds.

FEAR-IMPRINT PERIOD (8 to 11 weeks)

This occurs during the socialisation period, and it can be the cause of problems if it is not handled carefully. If a pup is exposed to a frightening or painful experience, it will lead to lasting impressions. Obviously, you will attempt to avoid frightening situations, such as your pup being bullied by a mean-spirited older dog, or a

IDEAS FOR SOCIALISATION

When you are socialising your Stafford, you want him to experience as many different situations as possible. Try out some of the following ideas, which will ensure your Stafford has an all-round education.

If you are taking on a rescued dog and have little knowledge of his background, it is important to work through a programme of socialisation. A young puppy soaks up new experiences like a sponge, but an older dog can still learn. If a rescued dog shows fear or apprehension, treat him in exactly the same way as you would treat a youngster who is going through the second fear-imprint period (see page?).

- Accustom your puppy to household noises, such as the vacuum cleaner, the television and the washing machine.
- Ask visitors to come to the door, wearing different types of clothing – for example, a hat or a long raincoat, or carrying a stick or an umbrella.
- If you do not have children at home, make sure your Stafford has a chance to meet and play with them. Go to a local park and watch children in the play area. You will not be able to take your Stafford inside the play area, but he will see children playing and will get used to their shouts of excitement.

- Attend puppy classes. These are designed for puppies between the ages of 12 to 20 weeks, and give puppies a chance to play and interact together in a controlled, supervised environment. Your vet will have details of a local class.
- Take a walk around some quiet streets, such as a residential area, so your Stafford can get used to the sound of traffic. As he becomes more confident, progress to busier areas.
- Go to a railway station. You don't have to get on a train if you don't need to, but your Stafford will have the chance to experience trains, people wheeling luggage, loudspeaker announcements, and going up and down stairs and over railway bridges.
- If you live in the town, plan a trip to the country. You can enjoy a day out and provide an opportunity for your Stafford to see livestock, such as sheep, cattle and horses.
- One of the best places for socialising a dog is at a country fair. There will be crowds of people, livestock in pens, tractors, bouncy castles, fairground rides and food stalls.
- When your dog is over 20 weeks of age, find a training class for adult dogs. You may find that your local training class has both puppy and adult classes.

not make your dog confront the thing that frightens him. Simply distract his attention, and give him something else to think about, such as obeying a simple command, such as "Sit" or "Down". This will give you the opportunity to praise and reward your dog, and will help to boost his confidence.

YOUNG ADULTHOOD AND MATURITY (1 to 4 years)

The timing of this phase is very much dependant on the size of the dog: the bigger the dog, the later it is. This period coincides with a dog's increased size and strength, mental as well as physical.

Some dogs, particularly those with a dominant nature, will test your leadership again and may also become aggressive towards other dogs.

Firmness and continued training are absolutely essential at this time so that your Staffordshire Bull Terrier continues to accept his status in the family pack.

TRAINING CLUBS

There are lots of training clubs to choose from. Your vet will probably have details of clubs in your area, or you can ask friends who have dogs if they attend a club. Alternatively, use the internet to find out more information. But how do you know if the club is any good?

Before you take your dog, ask if you can go to a class as an observer and find out the following:

- What experience does the instructor(s) have?
- Do they have experience with Staffords? It is important that your Stafford is treated in a positive manner, and is welcomed as a member of the class.
- Is the class well organised, and are the dogs reasonably quiet? (A noisy class indicates an unruly atmosphere, which will not be conducive to learning.)
- Are there are a number of classes to suit dogs of different ages and abilities?
- Are positive, reward-based training methods used?
- Does the club train for the Good Citizen Scheme (see page 104).

If you are not happy with the training club, find another one. An inexperienced instructor who cannot handle a number of dogs in a confined environment can do more harm than good.

THE ADOLESCENT STAFFORD

It happens to every dog – and every owner. One minute you have an obedient well-behaved youngster, and the next you have a boisterous adolescent who appears to have forgotten everything he learnt. This applies equally to males and females, although the type of adolescent behaviour, and its onset varies between individuals.

In most cases a Staffordshire Bull Terrier will hit adolescence at around 10-11 months, although this does vary between individuals. At this time, both male and female may become more assertive and harder to control.

Just like a teenager, an adolescent Stafford feels the need to flex his muscles and challenge the status quo. He may become very focused on his own desires and ignore your commands, or he may become disobedient and break house rules as he tests your authority and your role as leader. Your response must be firm, fair and consistent. If you show that you are a strong leader (see page 84) and are quick to reward good behaviour, your Stafford will accept you as his protector and provider.

As a Stafford matures, he will start to test his boundaries.

WHEN THINGS GO WRONG

Positive, reward-based training has proved to be the most effective method of teaching dogs, but what happens when your Stafford does something wrong and you need to show him that his behaviour is unacceptable? The old-fashioned school of dog training used to rely on the powers of punishment and negative reinforcement. A dog who raided the bin, for example, was smacked. Now we have learnt that it is not only unpleasant and cruel to hit a dog, it is also ineffective. If you hit a dog for stealing, he is more than likely to see you as the bad consequence of stealing, so he may raid the bin again, but probably not when you are around. If he raided the bin some time before you discovered it, he will be even more confused by your punishment, as he will not relate your response to his 'crime'.

A more commonplace example is when a dog fails to respond to a recall in the park. When the dog eventually comes back, the owner puts the dogs on the lead and goes straight home to punish the dog for his poor response. Unfortunately, the dog will have a different interpretation. He does not think: "I won't ignore a recall command because the bad consequence is the end of my play in the park." He thinks: "Coming to my owner resulted in the end of playtime – therefore coming to my owner has a bad consequence, so I won't do that again."

There are a number of strategies to tackle undesirable behaviour – and they have nothing to do with harsh handling.

Ignoring bad behaviour: A lot of undesirable behaviour in young Staffords is to do with over-exuberance. This trait is part of the breed's charm, but it can lead to difficult and sometimes dangerous situations. For example, a young Stafford that repeatedly jumps up at visitors is highly annoying, and, bearing in mind a Stafford's strength, he could even knock someone over. A Stafford is jumping up because he wants attention, so the best plan is to ignore him. Do not look at him, do not speak to him, and do not push him down – all these actions are rewarding for your Stafford. But someone who turns their back on him and offers no response is plain boring. The moment your Stafford has four feet on the ground, give him lots of praise and maybe a treat. If you repeat this often enough, the Stafford will learn that jumping up does not have any good consequences, such as getting attention. Instead he is ignored. However, when he has all four feet on the ground, he gets loads of attention. He links the action with the consequence, and chooses the action that is most rewarding. You will find that this strategy works well with all attention-seeking behaviour, such as barking, whining or scrabbling at doors. Being ignored is a worst-case scenario for a Stafford, so remember to use it as an effective training tool.

Stopping bad behaviour: There are occasions when you want to call an instant halt to whatever it is your Stafford is doing. He may have just jumped on the sofa, or you may have caught him red-handed in the rubbish bin. He has already committed the

DRASTIC ACTION

In an extreme situation, when you want to interrupt undesirable behaviour, and you know that a simple "No" will not do the trick, you can try something a little more dramatic. If you get a can and fill it with pebbles, it will make a really loud noise when you shake it or throw it. The same effect can be achieved with purpose-made training discs. The dog will be startled and stop what he is doing. Even better, the dog will not associate the unpleasant noise with you. This gives you the perfect opportunity to be the nice guy, calling the dog to you and giving him lots of praise.

'crime', so your aim is to stop him and to redirect his attention. You can do this by using a deep, firm tone of voice to say "No", which will startle him, and then call him to you in a bright, happy voice. If necessary, you can attract him with a toy or a treat. The moment your Stafford stops the undesirable behaviour and comes towards you, you can reward his good behaviour. You can back this up by running through a couple of simple exercises, such as a Sit or a Down, and rewarding with treats. In this way, your Stafford focuses his attention on you, and sees you as the greatest source of reward and pleasure.

PROBLEM BEHAVIOUR

If you have trained your Stafford from puppyhood, survived his adolescence and established yourself as a fair and consistent leader, you will end up with a brilliant companion dog. The Stafford is intelligent, affectionate, and is ready to co-operate. Most Staffordshire Bull Terriers share an exuberant love of life, and thrive on spending time with their owners.

However, problems may arise unexpectedly, or you may have taken on a rescued Stafford that has established behavioural problems. If you are worried about your Stafford and feel out of your depth, do not delay in seeking professional help. This is readily available, usually through a referral from your vet, or you can find out additional information on the internet (see Appendices for web addresses). An animal behaviourist will have experience in tackling problem behaviour and will be able to help both you and your dog.

SEPARATION ANXIETY

The Staffordshire Bull Terrier's outstanding quality is his love of people, and he will never take kindly to being shut away from his family. However, every dog should be brought up to accept short periods of separation from his owner, so that he tolerates the situation without becoming stressed. A new puppy should be left for short periods on his own, ideally in a crate where he cannot get up to any mischief. It is a good idea to leave him with a boredom-busting toy (see page 54) so he will be happily occupied in your absence. When you return, do not rush to the crate and make a huge fuss. Wait a few minutes, and then calmly go to the crate and release your dog, telling him how good he has been. If this scenario is repeated a number of times, your Stafford will soon learn that being left on his own is no big deal.

The behavioural problem most commonly encountered with rescued Staffords is separation anxiety. If a Stafford is left for lengthy periods, he may become very destructive if he is not confined. If he is confined, he may not have the opportunity to

If your Stafford is not used to being left alone, he may become anxious.

be destructive, but he may well develop other behavioural problems, such as continuous barking, soiling his crate, or even self-mutilating. This is a deeply distressing situation, and if you take on a Stafford with deep-seated separation anxiety, you may need to seek professional help. But to start with, you can try the following:

- Put up a baby-gate between adjoining rooms, and leave your dog in one room while you are in the other room. Your dog will be able to see you and hear you, but he is learning to cope without being right next to you. Build up the amount of time you can leave your dog in easy stages.
- Buy some boredom-busting toys and fill them with some tasty treats. Whenever you leave your dog, give him a food-filled toy so that he is busy while you are away.
- If you have not used a crate before, it is not too late to start. Make sure the crate is big and comfortable, and train your Stafford to get used to going in his crate while you are in the same room. Gradually build up the amount of time he spends in the crate, and then start leaving the room for short periods. When you return, do not make a fuss of your dog. Leave him for five or 10 minutes before releasing him so that he gets used to your comings and goings.
- Pretend to go out, putting on your coat and jangling keys,

but do not leave the house. An anxious dog often becomes hyped up by the ritual of leave taking, so this will help to desensitize him.
- When you go out, leave a radio or a TV on. Some dogs are comforted by hearing voices and background noise when they are left alone.
- Try to make your absences as short as possible when you are first training your dog to accept being on his own. When you return, do not fuss your dog,

rushing to his crate to release him. Leave him for a few minutes, and when you go to him remain calm and relaxed so that he does not become hyped up with a huge greeting.

If you take these steps, your dog should become less anxious, and, over a period of time, you should be able to solve the problem. However, if you are failing to make progress, do not delay in calling in expert help from a professional.

Accustom your Stafford to short periods of isolation, when you are still in sight, so that he learns to cope on his own.

DOMINANCE

If you have trained and socialised your Stafford correctly, he will know his place in the family pack and will have no desire to challenge your authority. As we have seen, adolescent dogs test the boundaries, and this is the time to enforce all your earlier training so your Stafford accepts that he is not top dog.

Staffordshire Bull Terriers are bold, fearless dogs, and some strong-minded individuals can become dominant if they sense weak leadership. This applies equally to male and female Staffords.

Dominance is expressed in many different ways, which may include the following:

- Showing lack of respect for your personal space. For example, your dog will barge through doors ahead of you or jump up at you.
- Getting up on to the sofa or your favourite armchair, and growling when you tell him to get back on the floor.
- Becoming possessive over a toy, or guarding his food bowl by growling when you get too close.
- Growling when anyone approaches his bed or when anyone gets too close to where he is lying.
- Ignoring basic commands.
- Showing no respect to younger members of the family, pushing amongst them, and completely ignoring them.
- Male dogs may start marking (cocking their leg) in the house.
- Aggression towards people, which is very rare in Staffords (see page 103).

If you see signs of your Stafford becoming too dominant, you must work at lowering his status so that he realises that you are the leader and he must accept your authority. Although you need to be firm, you also need to use positive training methods so that your Stafford is rewarded for the behaviour you want. In this way, his 'correct' behaviour will be strengthened and repeated.

There are a number of steps you can take to lower your Stafford's status. They include:

- Go back to basics and hold daily training sessions. Make sure you have some really tasty treats, or find a toy your Stafford really values and only bring it out at training sessions. Run through all the training exercises you have taught your Stafford. Make a big fuss of him and reward him when he does well. This will reinforce the message that you are the leader and that it is rewarding to do as you ask.
- Teach your Stafford something new; this can be as simple as learning a trick, such as shaking paws. Having something new to think about will mentally stimulate your Stafford, and he will benefit from interacting with you.
- Be 100 per cent consistent with all house rules – your Stafford must never sit on the

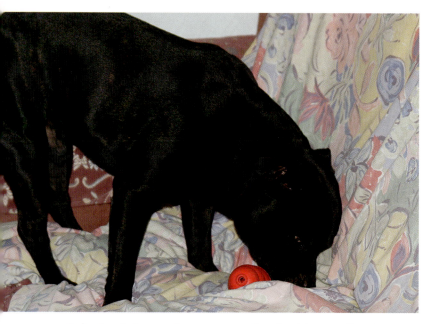

A dominant dog may become possessive about toys, or thwart your authority by jumping on the sofa.

sofa, and you must never allow him to jump up at you.

- If your Stafford has been guarding his food bowl, put the bowl down empty, and drop in a little food at a time. Periodically stop dropping in the food, and tell your Stafford to "Sit" and "Wait". Give it a few seconds, and then reward him by dropping in more food. This shows your Stafford that you are the provider of the food, and he can only eat when you allow him to.

- Make sure the family eats before you feed your Stafford. Some trainers advocate eating in front of the dog (maybe just a few bites from a biscuit) before starting a training session, so the dog appreciates your elevated status.

- Do not let your Stafford barge through doors ahead of you, or leap from the back of the car before you release him. You may need to put your dog on the lead and teach him to "Wait" at doorways, and then reward him for letting you go through first.

- If your Stafford is progressing well with his retraining programme, think about getting involved with a dog sport, such as agility or competitive obedience. This will give your Stafford a positive outlet for his energies. However, if your Stafford is still seeking to be dominant, or you have any other concerns, do not delay in seeking the help of an animal behaviourist.

Re-establish yourself as leader by lowering your dog's status. Here a Stafford is being told to "Wait" before he goes through the front door.

AGGRESSION

Aggression is a complex issue, as there are different causes and the behaviour may be triggered by numerous factors. It may be directed towards people, but far more commonly it is directed towards other dogs. Aggression in dogs may be the result of:

- Dominance (see page 102).
- Defensive behaviour: This may be induced by fear, pain or punishment.
- Territory: A dog may become aggressive if strange dogs or people enter his territory (which is generally seen as the house and garden).
- Intra-sexual issues: This is aggression between sexes – male-to-male or female-to-female.
- Parental instinct: A mother dog may become aggressive if she is protecting her puppies.

If a Stafford has been well bred, and well socialised from puppyhood, he may not be at all aggressive towards other dogs. In fact, Staffords form close friendships if they are reared

103

A Stafford will not back down from confrontation, so you will need to avoid situations where your Stafford may encounter a strange or unreliable dog.

GOOD CITIZEN SCHEME

This is a scheme run by the Kennel Club in the UK and the American Kennel Club in the USA. The schemes promote responsible ownership and help you to train a well-behaved dog who will fit in with the community. The schemes are excellent for all pet owners, and they are also a good starting point if you plan to compete with your Stafford when he is older. The KC and the AKC schemes vary in format. In the UK there are three levels: bronze, silver and gold, with each test becoming progressively more demanding. In the AKC scheme there is a single test.

Some of the exercises include:
- Walking on a loose lead among people and other dogs.
- Recall amid distractions.
- A controlled greeting where dogs stay under control while owners meet.
- The dog allows all-over grooming and handling by its owner, and also accepts being handled by the examiner.
- Stays, with the owner in sight, and then out of sight.
- Food manners, allowing the owner to eat without begging, and taking a treat on command.
- Sendaway – sending the dog to his bed.

The tests are designed to show the control you have over your dog, and his ability to respond correctly and remain calm in all situations. The Good Citizen Scheme is taught at most

together, particularly if it is a mixed-sex pair. The greater danger is meeting strange dogs, particularly if a strange dog comes into your dog's territory. Prevention is always the best course of action, and if your Stafford is intolerant of other dogs, never put him in a challenging situation. It only takes a second for a situation to escalate beyond your control.

If you have taken on an older, rescued dog, you will have little or no knowledge of his

background, and if he shows signs of aggression, the cause will need to be determined. In most cases, you would be well advised to call in professional assistance; if the aggression is directed towards people – which is very rare in Staffords – do not delay in seeking help.

NEW CHALLENGES

If you enjoy training your Stafford, you may want to try one of the many dog sports that are now on offer.

If your Stafford responds well to basic training, you may decide to take on some new challenges.

Showing is highly competitive but very rewarding if you reach the top.

training clubs. For more information, log on to the Kennel Club or AKC website (see Appendices).

SHOWING

In your eyes, your Stafford is the most beautiful dog in the world – but would a judge agree? Showing is a highly competitive sport, and the Stafford classes tend to be large. However, many owners get bitten by the showing bug, and their calendar is governed by the dates of the top showing fixtures.

To be successful in the show ring, a Stafford must conform as closely as possible to the Breed Standard, which is a written blueprint describing the 'perfect' Stafford (see Chapter Seven). To get started you need to buy a puppy that has show potential and then train him to perform in the ring. A Stafford will be expected to stand in show pose, walk for the judge in order to show off his natural movement, and to be examined by the judge. This involves a detailed hands-on examination, so your Stafford must be bombproof when handled by strangers.

Many breed clubs hold ringcraft classes, which are run by experienced showgoers. At these classes, you will learn how to handle your Stafford in the ring, and you will also find out about rules, procedures and show ring etiquette.

The best plan is to start off at some small, informal shows where you can practise and learn the tricks of the trade before graduating to bigger shows. It's a long haul starting in the very first puppy class, but the dream is to make your Stafford up into a Champion.

AGILITY, OBEDIENCE AND WORKING TRIALS

Several Staffordshire Bull Terriers compete on a regular basis in agility, obedience and working trials. Wendy Clewley's Tammy (Araidh Sweetest Taboo) is probably best known among show-going enthusiasts, as she was one of the stars of the team who gave demonstrations at breed club shows and at Crufts. In her prime, Tammy was one of the fastest 'medium' dogs in the UK and even beat the quickest Border Collie by 3 seconds over the same course! Tammy has a long list of training achievements, which include obedience, working trials and agility. She is also a registered therapy PAT Dog and a KC 'Gold' Good Citizen. However, it is agility at which she has excelled, a discipline that she apparently went into by accident. Tammy had been competing in obedience, and on the last day they were all taken to try their luck on the agility equipment. While some dogs had to be coaxed, Tammy just took to it straight away. In fact, the problem was trying to get her to stop!

It is recommended that agility training should not begin in earnest until your Stafford is 18 months of age. The intervening time can be spent socialising your dog and teaching basic obedience skills.

Marnie Wells has owned Staffords for 33 years and her dogs are a shining example of what can be achieved with this intelligent and trainable breed. Over the years she been extremely successful with her Staffords. Her first achievements were with Biggles (Arad Llewelyn Bren of Copyhold) who used to compete in obedience and working trials. Unfortunately, jumping was his nemesis so he never qualified, but he still managed to be placed on several occasions. He died in 2001 at nearly 10 years old. Marnie is very proud of the way he was mentioned in articles in the dog press, as he was such a wonderful character.

Bertie (Cyclone Sweetheart of Copyhold CDex UDex) was the first ever Stafford to gain the Utility Dog Excellent title (Udex) in working trials. She did some obedience and agility, in which sport she was placed over 200 times! She died in 2002 at nearly 11 years old. Marnie recalls the first time Bertie qualified UD at an open trial and won best track rosette – a wonderful result that she never thought a Stafford could achieve. Biggles and Bertie have the 'claim to fame' of appearing in the film *101 Dalmatians* and were also qualified PAT dogs.

Trilby (Libellula Lass of Copyhold CDex UDex) was a very successful trials dog, frequently winning best nose work and track trophies. She also did some agility with moderate success, and competed in obedience where she did very well and was certainly very popular and well known. She was in the Western obedience team at Crufts in 2003, and also did some photographic modelling. Trilby is retired now at 11, but still loves her training! The highlight of her competition career was the weekend when she won class A in obedience on the Saturday and Novice on the Sunday – a truly fantastic result. Trilby was also a qualified PAT dog.

It is, however, Marnie's latest protégé who is taking the obedience world by storm: Busby (Beraka Hurricane of Copyhold, NovEx CDex UDex) at only three years of age is the first Stafford to gain an Obedience Excellent Qualification since they were introduced by the Kennel Club at the beginning of 2006. He can now add the letters NovEx to the CDex and UDex after his name. To gain a Novice excellent, a dog has to gain points by being in the first four places in Novice Obedience classes (Novice in obedience is an extremely high standard). Busby has actually been in the rosettes (down to 6th) 18 times now. He is very consistent to the point where they even have Border Collie owners wishing Busby wasn't in their class, as he keeps beating them – quite a compliment! In Novice they have to do heelwork on and off the lead, a recall to front and retrieve a dumb-bell, and then there are stays: a one-minute sit and a two-minute down. To date, Busby has never broken a stay in obedience.

In working trials, the lowest stake is Companion Dog and to gain a CDex qualification you have to achieve 80 per cent of the marks in that stake at a Championship trial. This involves heelwork on and off lead at three different paces, a recall and a sendaway, which could be over 100 yards to a hedge or tree, a 10-

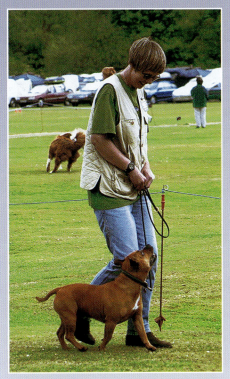

Trilby (Libellula Lass Of Copyhold Cdex Udex) doing her heelwork at an obedience show.
Twin Photographic.

An immaculate Present as part of the Novice Recall exercise.
Twin Photographic.

Busby (Beraka Hurricane of Copyhold NOVex, CDex, UDex) proves that Staffordshire Bull Terriers can win over other breeds by taking first place in a Championship CD stake.

minute down-stay and a two-minute sit-stay with the handlers out of sight. There is a search square 15 yards by 15 yards with three articles for the dog to find; these could range from a cork, a cartridge case, a piece of carpet/underlay to a spark plug – none of which the dog or handler has ever seen before – and a dumbbell retrieve. There are also three jumps to negoatiate: a 4 ft scale, a 2 ft clear jump and a 6 ft long jump. The work required for trials is much less formal than obedience, but extra commands are not allowed.

The next level in working trials is UDex (Utility Dog). This is where the immense fun of tracking starts. The dog has to follow a half-mile track and find two articles along the way, following the track pattern given to them by the judge. The track and articles will have been laid half an hour beforehand by a tracklayer. There is a bigger search square with four articles in it (they get more difficult at this level), and a steadiness to gunshot test. There is still heelwork off lead, a retrieve, a more difficult sendaway and a 10-minute down-stay. In addition, there are the jumps to complete. Busby's favourite exercise is the trials sendaway; he is apparently like a red cannon ball going out across the field!

To put Busby's achievements in a nutshell: he is the first ever Stafford male to gain UDex as well as CDex, the only Stafford to be asked to represent working trials at Crufts for two consecutive

years, and he was also part of the Obedience demonstration team. He and Marnie have been defeating some of the best professional handlers in the country in trials, he has learned to swim, and competed against Bloodhounds in a tracking match! All this in addition to the interviews and photo sessions. It goes without saying that any dog capable of doing all this is a very special dog indeed.

TRICKS

Jo-ann Essex demonstrates just what can be achieved with this truly versatile breed. Her dogs are very much the all–rounders, being successful as show dogs in addition to heelwork, agility and tricks, and, of course, family dogs. Jo-ann clicker trains her dogs, teaching them a new trick in as little as two days and once they know the tricks that they never forget. She doesn't go over the tricks unless they are training for a show; then she spends a week beforehand polishing the routine. The dogs' real love is agility and they train for that twice a week. Jo-ann has five Staffords, four of which are currently performing tricks: Suggs (Javawolf Red Bull) aged seven, Sumi-e (Rowellstaff Top Hatter with Javawolf) aged five, Bacon (Javawolf Mogwai) aged three, and finally, at the tender age of five months, Peppa (Javawolf Red Pepper).

Suggs and Bacon are the most adept and have formed a 'double act'. Their repertoire includes: Bacon propelling her pushchair with a toy dog in it, while Suggs

speciality is his 'dying act' – he falls on the floor when 'shot' with a toy gun, Jo-ann 'sneezes' and Suggs will take a handkerchief out of her back pocket, and they can both skateboard. However, the most popular trick is where Bacon sits in a toy car and Suggs pushes her along – that is guaranteed to bring the house down!

They have become Stafford celebrities and are in such great demand they have even had to employ their own agent! To date they have appeared in six TV adverts, in 'stills' for film posters and had numerous photo shoots for magazines. Jo-ann has appeared on *Blue Peter* twice: the first time with Sumi-e at the tender age of 11 weeks when Simon Thomas presented an item on training puppies. The second occasion was a mini 'Pup Idol' when Bacon was invited along with other breeds to demonstrate tricks. On this occasion she performed on her skateboard and received a Blue Peter Badge from presenters Matt Baker and Gethin Jones. Suggs and Bacon have met several TV personalities including Anthony Head (of *Buffy the Vampire Slayer* and *Little Britain* fame). In addition, they appeared on *This Morning* in 2005 as winners of the phone vote for the coveted title of 'Pup Idol'. They also have an excellent track record in competing at the Wag & Bone Show, having been semi-finalists in 2004 and runners-up in both 2005 and 2006.

Both Suggs and Bacon qualified to compete at Crufts on Terrier Day 2007 and were invited by the

Suggs (Javawolf Red Bull) proves how athletic a Staffordshire Bull Terrier can be.

Suggs pushing his wheel.

Photo: Alan Seymour.

Association of Pet Dog Trainers and a well-known dog food retailer to appear on their stand for the remaining three show days where – along with some other breeds – they performed 15-minute routines demonstrating their tricks. They received a fantastic reception and many members of the public commented that they just didn't think Staffords could be trained in such a way – yet more good publicity for the breed and an excellent opportunity to demonstrate their intelligence and versatility.

SUMMING UP

The Staffordshire Bull Terrier is a breed second to none – once you have owned a Stafford, no other breed will do. To get the best from your Stafford, you must be a firm and fair leader, and focus on bringing out your dog's qualities. A Stafford is clever, loving, and reliable; if you give him a good all-round education, he is a dog you can always be proud of.

THE PERFECT STAFFORD

Chapter 7

Seeking the perfect Stafford is rather like seeking the Holy Grail! To agree to what is the perfect dog/bitch we would need everyone to agree; even if one person disagreed (who would have to be an 'expert'), then doubt would be thrown on the matter. Over many years, more than I would care to tell you, I have seen quite a number of specimens that would be near to perfection as could be – but, of course, there are those who may disagree with me.

Some while ago, I was asked by the Kennel Club (along with others) to name the best dogs/bitches that I had ever judged. That was a difficult task because of the number of excellent specimens that I had judged over the years. In fact, I chose three specimens: two bitches and one dog but I could have included a number of

others, all very near to excellence, if not excellent. My three choices were: Ch. Bellglen Braws Best, Ch. Rendorn Deadly Nightshade, and Ch. Jodel's Mr Cool. I could have added many more, but I am reluctant to name them in case I miss out someone's dog or bitch.

So how do we go about attempting to breed the perfect Stafford? The first step would be to study the Staffordshire Bull Terrier Breed Standard. All Kennel Club registered breeds have their own Breed Standards, which have been composed by the pioneers of their breed. As a British breed, the Kennel Club Breed Standard is adopted by the Federation Cynologique Internationale (FCI), which governs countries outside UK and North America. The American Kennel Club (AKC) has its own Standard, but, in fact, there is only one clause that

is significantly different, and this refers to the Stafford's back (see Clause 9).

I have judged Staffords in many countries, and the main difference may be in a slight difference in weight and type. The main problem in a number of countries is the lack of specialist judges. All too often, the Stafford is judged by all-rounders. While all-rounders play an important role for any breed, it is also necessary for the specialist judge to play their part, to keep and improve type.

THE ORIGINAL BREED STANDARD

The Stafford Breed Standard was written by several fanciers in a pub in the Black Country, Staffordshire, hence the title of our breed. The main problem that these fanciers had was attempting to compose a Breed Standard that described both a

The original Breed Standard was written by a group of fanciers who met together in a pub.

show dog and the original and functional fighting dog – not, I imagine, an easy task. The purpose of this chapter is to explain the Breed Standard and to try to understand the reasons behind the original authors' thoughts when they sat down to compose it. We also have to remember that in 1935 there were probably not many Staffords that looked alike! So the original Breed Standard, accepted by the Kennel Club in 1936, was written to embrace as many dogs as possible, and was very different to the Standard that we use today.

1936 BREED STANDARD

APPEARANCE GENERAL
The Staffordshire Bull Terrier is a smooth coated dog, standing about 15 inches to 18 inches high at the shoulder. He should give the impression of great strength for his size, and although muscular should be active and agile.
We should note the changes in height, otherwise similar wording to the current Standard.

HEAD
Short, deep through, broad skull, very pronounced cheek
muscles, distinct stop, short foreface, mouth level.
Very similar wording, but note the mouth description – there is no mention of the scissor bite.

EARS
Rose, half prick and prick; these three to be preferred, full drop to be penalised.
Note, this Standard allows a prick ear!

EYES
Dark.
Note that there is little description of the eye as compared to the modern Standard.

NECK
Should be muscular and rather short.
Little change here from the current Standard.

BODY
Short back, deep brisket, light in loins, with forelegs set rather wide apart to permit of chest development.
Very different to the modern Breed Standard. Now there is no mention of short back or rather light in loins. This Standard does not mention a level topline.

FRONT LEGS
Straight, feet well padded, to turn out a little and showing no weakness at pasterns.
Worded a little differently, but has the same up-to-date meaning.

HIND LEGS

Hindquarters well muscled, let down at the hocks like a Terrier.

It is interesting, the reference of the word terrier; otherwise very similar in meaning.

COAT

Short, smooth and close to skin.

Very similar to the present Standard.

TAIL

The tail should be of medium length tapering to a point and carried rather low; it should not curl much and may be compared with an old fashioned pump handle.

The same as the present Standard.

WEIGHT

Dogs 28lbs to 38lbs. Bitches 4lbs less

The weight for dogs is the same now, but for bitches it is 11-15.4 kg.

COLOUR

May be any shade of Brindle, Black, White, Fawn or Red, or any of these colours with White.
Black and Tan and Liver not to be encouraged.

Again very much the same, except in our present Standard black and tan and liver is described as highly undesirable.

FAULTS TO BE PENALISED

Dudley nose, light or pink eyes (rims), tail too long or badly

Over the years the Staffordshire Bull Terrier developed a similarity of type and appearance to create the breed we know today.

curled, badly undershot or overshot mouths.
Very different from our present Standard, which does not mention any particular point.

It is very interesting that they were prepared to accept bad mouths, unless they were **badly undershot or overshot**. It has taken breeders many years to virtually rid the breed of this problem, although occasionally bad mouths appear in a litter.

It is worth noting that the 1936 Standard had only 13 clauses, whereas the present Standard has 17 clauses. When the breed was first exhibited in

the show ring, the method of judging was very different, as exhibits were judged to a scale of points:

SCALE OF POINTS

General appearance, coat and condition	15
Head	30
Neck	10
Body	25
Legs and feet	15
Tail	5
Total	100

This system has been abandoned for many years, but it is of interest that 30 points were awarded to the head, which seems to make our breed a 'head breed'.

The Breed Standard has been altered two or three times over the years – in 1948 and again in 1978. However, once the initial Breed Standard is agreed upon, it becomes the property of the Kennel Club, and it cannot be altered or changed without the permission of the Kennel Club, along with 100 per cent agreement of all the 18 Stafford breed clubs.

UNDERSTANDING THE BREED STANDARD

So what is a Breed Standard? The only way to explain this is to liken it to an engineer's blueprint, when he or she constructs or assembles a piece of engineering. The engineer will constantly consult this document to make sure that the precise and accurate measurements are followed. Perhaps judges should have a copy of their particular Breed Standard on the judging table to consult if necessary.

The Breed Standards are a little different from the engineer's blueprint in that we, the breeders and judges, are given a little latitude, and there can be various interpretations. For example, the description of the head refers to a '**short foreface**', which could vary widely according to individual interpretation. However, I believe that most serious and responsible breeders do try to breed to the Standard.

An outstanding Staffordshire Bull Terrier showing overall balance and great strength for its size.

DETAILED ANALYSIS

1 GENERAL APPEARANCE
Smooth coated, well balanced, of great strength for his size. Muscular, active and agile.

This is a very important clause – in a few words it completely describes the dog. It is telling us that this is a powerful, agile, dog. The word 'balance' is of paramount importance and it sums up the dog, 'a lot of dog in a small space'.

2 CHARACTERISTICS
Traditionally of indomitable courage and tenacity. Highly intelligent and affectionate, especially with children.

This has to be the most important clause of the Standard, and this is the only Breed Standard, with the exception of the Chesapeake Bay Retriever, that specifically states **affectionate with children**, so reliability and affection must be number one in breeders' and judges' approach to this breed. A dog that is not totally reliable should never be bred from, regardless.

The **highly intelligent** part is not always recognised. As we have seen in Chapter 6, Staffords excel in many canine activities, such as working as therapy dogs and competing in agility and obedience.

3 TEMPERAMENT
Bold, fearless, and totally reliable.

The Staffordshire Bull Terrier relates closely to people, which is a hallmark of the breed.

The correct proportions of the head with a broad skull, a pronounced stop, and a short foreface.

Again, we have another reference to the dog's attitude towards human beings – his reliability, making him among the foremost of dependable companion and family dogs. Clauses 2 and 3 are the Staffordshire Bull Terrier's most endearing features or virtues, and breeders and judges must guard it at all costs. It is a pity that the media does not take the trouble to present the breed in its true light.

4 HEAD AND SKULL
Short, deep through with broad skull. Very pronounced stop, short foreface, nose black.

Probably the most controversial clause in the Standard is the **short foreface**. The point usually made is: how long is long, or how long is a piece of string? This clause is very clear in describing the length and depth of the skull, i.e. a short, deep, broad skull. We

must be aware of exaggerations in this part of the dog because of the words 'short and deep'. We have to decide what the authors of the Breed Standard were trying to describe, or what they actually meant: how deep is deep and how short is short?

The answer is quite simple. In the 1930s the most popular house dogs were the Fox Terrier and the Airedale Terrier, both carrying long forefaces. It is therefore not difficult to understand that short in foreface can only mean shorter than the two terriers' type of forefaces. The ideal ratio, accepted by most people is two-thirds skull to one-third foreface. As with a deep, short and broad skull, we are not looking for a Bulldog or a Mastiff, we are seeking a happy medium (or 'not too much, and not too little'). In my view, the authors knew what they were doing and were simply looking for a balanced and active dog combining both 'Bull and Terrier'.

Some years ago, it was fairly common to see a Stafford head and skull with a ratio of almost half and half, with a shallow stop. However, heads have improved considerably over the last 20 years, although some will point out that many heads are too short in the foreface, with the possible result of breathing problems.

5 EYES
Dark preferred but may bear some relation to coat colour. Round, of medium size, and set to look straight ahead. Eye rims dark.

I believe that correct eye colour and placement is essential to capture the desired and correct Stafford expression, particularly the correct placement. Incorrect placement will give the Stafford a foreign expression. The actual colour of the eye can vary, but a dark eye on any coloured dog is an attractive and desirable sight, and a very light eye on a dark or black brindle is disconcerting to most judges.

Dark eye rims can be a problem on white dogs and it may take time for the pigmentation to spread around the eye rim. Sometimes the pigmentation does not spread around the eye, and such a dog will be liable to be penalised by the judge. What can be helpful to improve, or keep good pigmentation, is a regular supply of green vegetables, such as cabbage, spinach, and spring greens, and giving a white dog iron-based homoeopathic remedies, such as seaweed powder or elderberry tablets.

A rose ear enhances the Stafford head.

6 EARS

Rose or half pricked, not large or heavy. Full, drop or pricked ears highly undesirable.

A neat, small rose ear on a Stafford certainly is very desirable. It enhances the head, and is essential for the original purpose of the breed (in a dog fight ears had to be well tucked back so they were not targets). Sadly, this type of ear is not as common as it once was. Many people do not realise that a half prick ear is allowed, and, over the years, I have seen dogs penalised for this very type of ear. Heavy or large ears certainly spoil the expression of the dog. When breeding Staffords, poor ears can prove difficult to improve.

7 MOUTH

Lips tight and clean. Jaws strong, teeth large, with a perfect, regular and complete scissor bite, i.e. upper teeth closely overlapping the lower teeth and set square to the jaws.

A very important clause; it would be very difficult to win in the show ring if a dog does not have a scissor bite.

Back in the 1960s and 1970s, undershot or overshot mouths were a problem for the breed. Most litters in those days usually contained two or even three

The Breed Standard asks for strong jaws and big teeth, set in a scissor bite.

pups with mouth problems. However, judges were very strict, often penalising the merest hint of a mouth fault, and this has paid dividends, because the mouth problem has largely disappeared.

The main problem today is misplaced canines, often mistakenly referred to as 'inverted' canines (dictionary meaning: 'to turn upside down'!). I am sure that this serious fault can be rectified with sensible and careful breeding, and close examination while dogs are being judged.

Large teeth are very desirable in the Stafford, and some of the mouth problems over the years have come from small teeth.

8 NECK
Muscular, rather short, clean in outline gradually widening towards the shoulders.

We are back to 'short', or 'rather short'. This piece of the Standard needs a little thought. A very short neck is not wanted nor is a longish neck. It is simply a matter of balance: if it looks long, then it is long; if it looks short, then it is short. If, however, it neither looks long nor short, then it must be correct! To see the neck flowing to the shoulders is a pleasing sight to all good judges. Good muscle is also essential on the neck of the Stafford.

9 FOREQUARTERS
Legs straight and well boned, set rather wide apart, showing no weakness at the pasterns, from which point feet turn out a little. Shoulders well laid back with no looseness at elbow.

A good description of a dog, but we return to the 'rather wide apart', and how wide is rather wide? Again, we can use the same simple test: if it looks wide, it is too wide; if it looks narrow, then it is too narrow.

I believe that 'well boned' is vitally important, because a Stafford with poor bone does not really look like a real Stafford. It is essential that both the judge and the breeder look for good bone, although, of course, heavy bone is equally undesirable.

'Feet turn out a little', is another contentious part of the Standard, as dogs with feet turned out could be penalised, and often are penalised. I believe it was included in the original Standard (1935) because in the early 1930s many Staffords may

The front legs are straight and well boned.

The body is short coupled with a level topline.

have had poor fronts, which would encourage the feet to turn out. I believe that the authors of the Breed Standard would have wanted to include all the dogs around at that time (particularly those gentlemen sitting in that pub who owned such dogs), even if they were not top-class specimens, and they would have wanted as many dogs as possible to support the new venture and take part in the showing side.

9 BODY
Close-coupled, with level topline, wide front, deep brisket, well sprung ribs; muscular and well defined.

This particular clause actually contradicts Clause 8, where it asks for a front '**rather wide apart**', whereas this clause asks for a '**wide front**'. In this instance, a judge has to make a personal interpretation.

A level topline is essential to give a dog an attractive outline. There is a problem in the breed today with too many dogs carrying poor toplines. They are usually 'sway backs', meaning that that the back falls away towards the shoulders, or 'roached backs', as seen in a Whippet or Bedlington Terrier. Sadly, these serious faults are commonplace in the breed today, because when a dog is 'set up',

the topline may appear to be level and acceptable to the eye. It is, therefore, essential to judge dogs while they are on the move, to ensure that this fault is clearly noted.

The original Standard asked for a **short back**, but that description disappeared from the Standard a while ago. However, there are judges who still look for a short back, and I have seen this point written (as a virtue) in show critiques. But as long as the dog is balanced, we do not have to look for this short back.

Interestingly, the American Kennel Club Breed Standard does ask for the short back.

The legs are parallel when viewed from behind.

essential part of their anatomy. The hindquarters are the driving force and power for a Stafford, and good judges will always look for this vital part of the Staffordshire Bull Terrier and penalise accordingly. If this essential virtue is ignored, then it is possible that we will lose it forever.

11 FEET

Well padded, strong and of medium size. Nails black in solid coloured dogs.

A straightforward explanation. Weak, and thin feet, splayed feet, longish toes and large feet are very unattractive, but sometimes poor feet can be improved a little by road walking. Regular nail trimming can improve the way the nails grow, which can affect the feet, i.e. some nails grow sharply downwards, while others grow forwards, and this can affect the look of the feet.

Keeping nails black can present a problem, often in the winter months with nails looking brown or a lighter colour. A regular course of iron-based products (as mentioned previously) may help with this.

10 HINDQUARTERS

Well muscled, hocks well let down with stifles well bent. Legs parallel when viewed from behind.

'**Hocks well let down**' often present a problem, because, in my view, it is not terribly descriptive. All points in a Standard should be easily

understandable, even if they are open to interpretation, and this point is not as clear as it might be. It really needs a diagram to clarify.

Many clauses contain the description '**well muscled**' so it shows how important muscle is to the breed. '**Stifles well bent**' is easily understandable, but sadly many Staffords today lack this

12 TAIL

Medium length, low set, tapering to a point and carried rather low. Should not curl much and may be likened to an old fashioned pump handle.

This clause is very easy to understand, but too many dogs and bitches nowadays carry their tails up in the air or even over their backs. In the 1980s, you rarely saw Staffords with high-set or gay tails, and it gives concern to many people. If we ignore this unattractive and ugly fault, we could lose the traditional and typical old fashioned pump handled tail. I feel certain that the original authors of the Breed Standard would be horrified by the gay tails seen in the ring today.

Trimming is a positive way to improve the appearance of the tail, and a correct, low, pump handled tail is the finishing touch to a good specimen. Gay tails are an unattractive sight in the ring, and certainly spoil the look of an otherwise excellent dog.

GAIT/MOVEMENT
Free, powerful and agile with economy of effort. Legs moving parallel when viewed from front or rear. Discernible drive from hindlegs.

Movement was not included in the original Breed Standard, and in my opinion, dogs moved more soundly than some of the dogs today.

It is essential to assess the dog when on the move, because the moving dog exposes any number of undesirable faults, i.e. poor topline, unsoundness, gay tail (all hidden on a 'standing and set up dog'). A dog that moves correctly clearly shows that he is well constructed, and then the judge can look at the other essentials.

13 COAT
Smooth, short and close.

Movement should be free, powerful and agile.

A simple and easily understood clause. Most Stafford coats are usually smooth and close, although sometimes we find dogs with coarse coats, often on a black or black brindle. Breeding red to brindle (or brindle to red) can improve the texture of coats.

We are rather spoilt in the matter of coats because the breeds with long or double coats have to take some time to prepare their dogs, but, even so, some attention to the coat should be given, particularly to the show Stafford. It is a good idea to bath the dog a day or two before a show and perform some grooming just before he is taken into the ring.

THE COLOUR RANGE

Mahogany brindle.

Tiger brindle.

15 COLOUR
Red, fawn, white, black or blue or any one of these colours and white. Any shade of brindle with white. Black and tan or liver highly undesirable.

All these various colours certainly make this breed unique; there are nearly 40 colours, or combinations of colours. But looking at the contemporary Staffords in the show ring, you could be forgiven for assuming that the breed consisted of black and/or black brindles, with the odd (usually unplaced) red! It may surprise some to learn that there are so many colours and variations of colour. They include the following:

- Red, dark red, chestnut colour red
- Fawn, several shades of fawn.
- Black brindle
- Red brindle
- Mahogany brindle
- Tiger brindle, often confused with red brindle
- Fawn brindle
- Black
- Red and white pied*

Fawn and white.

Red fawn.

- Various shades of brindle and white pied*
- Black and white pied*
- White – and all the solid colours with white
- Blue – blues are quite rare, and a true blue will have good pigmentation with dark eyes

(* A pied is a mixture of any colour and white, but white must be the major colour.)

It saddens me that many of these colours are in a small minority. If we, as breeders and judges, sit back and watch the breed become mainly black or black brindles, we will lose one of the many traditional and attractive features of our breed.

In the early 1960s and 1970s, most litters would contain reds, various shades of brindles, and pieds, and in the show ring you would see a wide selection of colours being judged in every class. At the present time, I have seen classes of 20 or 30 Staffords with only two or three reds or light brindles entered. Some exhibitors who own reds are often reluctant to enter their dogs under certain judges, who appear not to consider placing

Black brindle.

Red and white.

PIGMENTATION

This is not mentioned very much in the Breed Standard, but it is a very important requirement for our perfect dog. You can often see specimens in the show ring that have poor pigmentation. The obvious signs are: circles around the eyes (referred to as 'spectacles'), lack of hair between the hind legs, or sometimes a washed-out colour of brindle often mistaken for blue.

Ideally we would want black toenails, a black mask on a red dog, dark eyes, and/or some blackness around the mouth. Then we would be looking for that extra bit of class that defines the 'real McCoy', or makes him the perfect dog.

reds. These judges are certainly not judging to the Standard!

15 FAULTS

Any departure from the foregoing points should be considered a fault and the seriousness with which the fault should be regarded should be in exact proportion to its degree.

A very important clause, which should be read very carefully so that we fully understand its implications. Fault judging is easy, and it is the means in which poor judges take refuge. There are

Red and white pied.

Brindle pied.

obviously more serious faults than others: poor construction must be the most obvious fault to penalise, as is lack of type. The rest is mainly a matter of commonsense. In good-quality specimens, a judge has to be kind to minor faults, as excellent specimens usually do carry minor blemishes.

NOTE
Male animals should have two apparently normal testicles descended into the scrotum.

AIMING FOR PERFECTION
We have bred our litter to the Breed Standard, so what else can we do to produce the perfect dog?

FAULT JUDGING
The Faults clause must be treated in a responsible way. Any fool (and they often do) can 'fault judge'; it is the easiest way for some. The way to approach this is to be kind to faults, except the most serious:

- Lack of type
- Unsoundness
- Bad temperament
  These three faults should be treated with the utmost severity.

EXAGGERATIONS
Although all the necessary basic requirements should be foremost in our minds, there is another important factor that we should not lose sight of – a factor that can be staring us in the face, yet can be missed or ignored. This factor can creep up on the unwary, and by the time you become aware, it can be too late. I refer to the dangers of exaggerations that can, and has, overtaken other breeds. The classic examples that stand out are the Bulldog, Bloodhound and the German Shepherd Dog. It is worth remembering that the

In the show ring every dog is given a hands-on examination to assess conformation.

problems that these breeds suffer did not occur overnight.

How could exaggeration affect the Staffordshire Bull Terrier? We know that the Stafford is considered to be an unspoilt dog, so how can we spoil it? The Stafford could be affected by over-wide fronts, over-large skulls, be over-boned, or even under-boned, and have too much substance. Certainly, too short a foreface could affect the breathing, making the dog resemble a Boston Terrier, not forgetting the bulbous eye that is sometimes seen.

These particular points could, over time, lead to exaggerations and spoil an otherwise unspoilt dog.

BREEDING WITH ACCEPTED COLOURS

To preserve the traditional colours of the Staffordshire Bull Terrier (the red/fawn/mahogany/ shades of brindle), it is necessary to use red to brindle and vice versa. Red to red done consistently could lose the richness and depth of red, so a dark brindle should be introduced when planning the

breeding programme.

A well-known successful breeder, Teresa Miller (Rellim), who sadly passed away many years ago, always endeavoured to breed red to brindle at every mating. This certainly ensured good coat texture and colours.

Many breeders are reluctant to use red dogs on their dark/black brindles for fear of undesirable colours resutling. Of course, there is always that possibility, but the rewards gained in good colours and coat texture make it a worthwhile attempt.

It is the Staffordshire Bull Terriers that conform most closely to the Breed Standard that will receive the top placings.

SUMMARY

I have spent a lifetime studying the Staffordshire Bull Terrier, and I still find the breed completely fascinating. The Breed Standard is not a lengthy document, but there is so much to learn if you take the time to study it, and to develop a eye for what the 'perfect' Staffordshire Bull Terrier should look like. I hope my analysis will help the novice to understand what the Standard is trying to tell us, and will bring to the attention of breeders, judges and exhibitors alike the problems that our breed is experiencing, such as poor toplines, weak hindquarters, lack of bone and faulty movement. It is only by paying close heed to the Breed Standard that we can preserve this truly great breed for the enjoyment of future generations.

HAPPY AND HEALTHY

Chapter 8

A Staffordshire Bull Terrier is courageous and will enjoy life if he is given opportunities for exercise and a chance to use his mind. It is your job to stimulate your Stafford's interest in play and 'work'. As an all-purpose family dog, the Staffordshire Bull Terrier has proved his ability in providing companionship but will need lots of energetic activity to keep healthy. There should be opportunities for stimulating walks to provide exercise; he must be fed a balanced diet to maintain a fit body; and he needs veterinary care with necessary vaccinations and parasite control.

Visits to the veterinary surgeon are required for vaccinations, at which time it is usual to make a physical examination of the dog for any undisclosed disease. In between times, daily grooming of the dog provides the opportunity to get to know the dog's coat and the body structure, so that signs of illness can be detected earlier than if left until the dog is in pain or refusing his food. Improved diet and routine vaccinations are contributing to a much longer life for all domestic animals, but the owner of the dog has a role to play in everyday health care.

It is very important that you really get to know your dog, as you will more easily identify when the dog is not right or 'off colour' and seek appropriate veterinary advice. It is also important to know the signs of a healthy dog when you go to buy a puppy or perhaps purchase an adult dog. Visits to the vet should be made whenever an abnormality may be detected. By using pet insurance, the cover provided gives the opportunity for extensive tests and procedures to be undertaken on dogs. Before choosing a policy it is important to assess what the insurance company is offering and what sort of limits are put on expense, age limit or hereditary disorders requiring veterinary attention.

The purchaser of a puppy will wish to ensure as good a start in life for the pup as possible. As well as the health inspection the veterinary surgeon will give the animal at the first visit prior to vaccination, information should be obtained from the breeder on the health status of the puppy's closest relatives. X-rays for hip scoring may have been performed on both parents and you can ask for these. Eye examinations before breeding are often required and the Kennel Club offers registration of dogs in various breeds where known hereditary eye diseases occur. Tests for hereditary cataract using DNA are available for the Staffordshire Bull Terrier and a breeder may be able to give

To begin with, puppies receive immunity through their mother's milk.

reassurance that the parents of a puppy are not carriers. There are over 20 condition listed as hereditary for Staffordshire Bull Terriers, but it is not possible to recognise many of these until they occur, as they may be 'late in onset'.

ROUTINE HEALTH CARE

VACCINATIONS
One of the greatest advances in canine practice in the last 50 years has been the development of effective vaccines to prevent diseases. Within living memory dogs died from fits after distemper virus infections, and in the last 20 years a high number of puppies had parvovirus, which resulted in many fatalities until a vaccine was developed. The routine use of a multiple component vaccine to protect against canine distemper,

infectious canine hepatitis, parvovirus and leptospirosis is accepted, but there are still local differences in the age at which a puppy receives his first injection or 'shot'.

The timing for the primary vaccine course is based on an understanding of when the immunity, provided by the mother, declines to a level that will not interfere with the pup's immune response. Canine vaccines currently in use in the UK have recommendations for the final dose of the primary course to be given at 10 or 12 weeks of age; and boosters after the first year are usual. With dogs that spend time outdoors, this annual dose is especially necessary for protection against potentially fatal leptospirosis, which occurs in water and where rats have been present.

The length of protection

provided after two injections for the puppy is not significantly greater than 12 months (challenges after this date result in shedding of leptospires), and for some vaccines it is even considered less than 12 months. For protection against the other viruses, a minimum of three years is possible, and annual boosters are less essential. However, further booster vaccination is recommended at intervals, decided by the vet, who has a local knowledge of disease incidence.

Kennel cough is a distressing infectious disease usually acquired from airborne contact with other dogs, especially those stressed when visiting dog shows or boarding kennels. There are several vaccines available and, again, advice should be obtained from the vet as to which type of protection is appropriate to the dog's exposure.

Rabies vaccine is necessary for all dogs leaving the United Kingdom, but is routine in many countries, as is the vaccine for Lyme disease in the US, where it should be discussed with the veterinarian.

(See Ailments A-Z for more information on these infectious diseases.)

WORMING AND PARASITE CONTROL
Routine worming every three months is obligatory to reduce the risk of infection of susceptible humans handling the dog. De-wormers are necessary for puppies as well as for adult dogs.

Many puppies are infested with roundworms, but some breeders will start worming the pregnant bitch to reduce the risk to the newborn pups. Worming of a puppy from two weeks, repeated at regular intervals, is advised. Roundworms, hookworms, tapeworms and whipworms present different threats, while heartworms (which can result from the bite of an infected mosquito) are a particular problem of the south-east Atlantic and Gulf Coasts of the USA, and, with climate change, has become an increasing threat in the UK. Those dog owners planning to take their pet to mainland Europe should know that heartworm is endemic in the Mediterranean area of France, but, with global warming, is slowly spreading northwards.

A single flea on the dog's coat can cause persistent scratching and restlessness. Many effective anti-flea preparations are now available – some as tablets by mouth, some as coat applications, and some as residual sprays to apply to carpets and upholstery frequented by cats as well as dogs. Lice, fleas, and mites (those that burrow under the skin and those that live on the surface) may all cause disease and are not always recognised. The exception is ticks, which become large and visible as they gorge themselves with the dog's blood. A thorough grooming of the dog each day will detect many of these parasites, and suitable protective products should be applied as needed. These may be supplied as a

Worming is essential for all puppies, as most will carry roundworm.

powder, a shampoo, a spot-on insecticide or a spray.

DIET AND EXERCISE FOR HEALTH
Some Staffords are naturally lean and, although they look as though they are underweight, they are perfectly fit, even though they appear to carry little body fat. More sedentary Staffords may be inclined to put on weight as they get older.

It is a good idea to weigh dogs on a regular basis; the dog that appears thin but is still actively fit has fewer reserves to fall back on, and weighing on a weekly basis can detect further weight loss before any disastrous change can occur. Each dog should have an ideal weight and, within a narrow range, the correct weight for the dog will act as a guide.

Obesity has become a major concern. Appetite suppressants, prescribed by the vet, can be

used as part of an overall weight management programme.

GROOMING
The Staffordshire Bull Terrier's coat should be short, smooth and close. Too much indoor confinement, with warm temperatures, can lead to the loss of undercoat and less hair density for waterproof outdoor protection.

Regular brushing and grooming is important for a number of reasons. It stimulates the skin and also provides an opportunity for closer inspection of the underlying skin:
• Grooming stimulates the hair growth stage known as anagen by the removal of dead, shedding hairs. This helps to prevent bald patches.
• The removal of eye discharge, or any other form of discharge, prevents the coat matting as well as preventing skin irritation.

GROOMING CHECKLIST

The close inspection of the animal during grooming assists in the early recognition of problems. During grooming, pay attention to any bony prominences, skin folds, feet and claws, eyes and ears, mouth and teeth, anus, vulva and prepuce. Check for traces of fleas or ticks attached to the skin. When grooming the dog, always make a point of checking the ears both inside and out. The start of ear trouble can be detected by observing the way the dog holds his head and the use of your nose to smell out trouble! Bathing may be needed either to eradicate and control ectoparasites or to cleanse the coat and remove smells, as well as for cosmetic reasons, such as improving a dog's appearance before a show.

The pads of the feet should feel quite soft to the touch and not leathery or horny (hyperkeratinised). The pigment of the foot pads is often similar to the nose colour. Between the toes is an area of skin that is hairy and contains sebaceous glands used for scent marking. Occasionally, cysts and swellings develop if the glands become blocked. The skin between the toes is very sensitive to chemical burns, and some alkaline clay soils will provoke inflammation with lameness known as 'pedal eczema'.

The nails should be of even length and not split at the ends after being left to grow too long. If the nails are too long, they need to be clipped, taking care to avoid hurting the dog by cutting into the quick. Exercise on hard, concrete surfaces is normally sufficient to keep nails at a reasonable length; tarmac roads and tarred pavements do not provide enough friction to wear down nails. Dewclaws, if present, are not a disadvantage to the dog. But they will need to be trimmed if they grow in a circle, as they can penetrate the flesh, causing an infected wound.

A-Z OF COMMON AILMENTS

ALLERGIES

Allergies are now a common diagnosis for many dogs with skin or intestinal disorders. The condition results from an inappropriate immune response by the dog to an antigen substance, either in the food or inhaled through the nose. A process of eliminating possible antigens in the diet, or in the environment, may help to find a cause – and there are commercial diets available that may help. Medication can be used to suppress the allergic response and both antihistamines and steroids may be tried before the most suitable treatment is found.

ANAL DISORDERS

Modern diets are often blamed for the high incidence of dogs needing their anal 'glands' squeezed out at regular intervals. These glands are actually little sacs just at the edge of the anus opening, and they contain strong-smelling, greasy substances used to 'mark' the freshly passed faeces for other animals to recognise. Over-production of the fluid causes the dog discomfort, and, when a suitable floor surface is available, the dog will then 'scoot' along, leaving a trail of odorous matter.

Occasionally, infection of the gland will alter the smell, and this may result in other dogs being attracted to a female-type odour. A course of antibiotics can have a direct benefit on this apparent behaviour problem. Abscesses of the anal sacs are very painful; they may require drainage, although often they swell and burst on their own with a sudden blood-stained discharge. Flushing out and antibiotics may be required as treatment.

Other glands around the anus may become cancerous, and attention is drawn to these if bleeding occurs. Adenomata are tumours found in the older male dog and require veterinary attention before bleeding occurs.

ARTHRITIS

This joint disease was once often found after an infection, but now the condition is usually either due to joint wear and tear (degenerative) or as a result of an immune system reaction – rheumatoid arthritis and idiopathic arthritis being examples. At first, degenerative arthritis improves with exercise, but afterwards the dog will stiffen, and, on bending the joint, often a painful grating 'crepitus' can be found.

Treatment will be aimed at keeping the dog mobile and any excess weight should be lost. Anti-inflammatory medication on a daily basis will remove pain and discomfort. Blood tests and X-rays may be needed for investigating arthritis. Some owners have good results with supplements, such as the glycosaminoglycans.

ATOPY

Sometimes known as inhalant allergy, atopy is associated with many chronic skin diseases characterised by pruritus – a sensation within the skin that provokes the Stafford to have a desire to scratch, lick, chew or rub himself to alleviate the irritation. Not as common as in some other breeds, it may require specific tests and medication to relieve the itching. The signs do not usually develop until one to three years.

The Staffordshire Bull Terrier is generally a healthy breed, but it is important to be aware of ailments that may affect your dog.

The characteristic roughened, itchy, oozing skin may be caused by the immune reactions to various allergens, such as fleas or pollen. There is an indication of an inherited tendency, and there is often a seasonal change if specific pollens are the cause.

AURAL HAEMATOMA

This is where the ear flap suddenly swells due to internal bleeding between the skin and the ear cartilage. It can be distressing to the Stafford and will cause repeated head shaking. Bleeding is usually the result of fierce scratching with the hind toes, perhaps triggered by a tingling inside the ear canal. Grass seeds or other foreign bodies entering the tube of the outer ear will also provoke such scratching. Ear mites, acquired from cats, can have a similar effect.

Treatment of aural haematoma usually involves drainage of the

blood under general anaesthesia and implementing measures to stop the dog shaking his head, thus preventing further bleeding. See also Otitis externa.

BRONCHITIS

Inflammation of the breathing tubes is often the result of a virus or a bacterial infection, but irritant gases and dust can also be the cause of repeated coughing. Kennel cough is the most common infection, which results in sticky mucus clinging to the base of the windpipe (trachea) and the tubes entering the lungs (bronchii). Coughing similar to bronchitis is seen in older dogs associated with congestive heart failure, which may occur with a failing heart muscle and fluid accumulating in the lungs.

Antibiotics may be prescribed by the vet to reduce the bronchitis signs and the risk of further bacterial infection leading

Arthritis is more likely to affect the Staffordshire Bull Terrier in old age.

to generalised pneumonia. Cough suppressants and 'antitussives' can be used to suppress a persistent cough, but should not be used if there is bronchopneumonia. Steam inhalations, often with a volatile oil, have been used to relieve a dry cough.

BURNS AND SCALDS
First-aid measures require immediate cooling of the skin, which can be done by pouring cold water over the affected area repeatedly for at least 10 minutes. Some scalds, where hot water or oil has been spilt, penetrate the coat. They may not be recognised until a large area of skin and hair peels away, after heat has killed the surface skin cells. As these injuries are considered to be very painful, analgesics (pain relief) should be obtained and in anything but the smallest injured area, antibiotics

would be advised, as secondary bacteria will multiply on exposed raw surfaces.

Bandages and dressings are not a great help, but clingfilm has been used in some situations. Clipping the hair away over a large area surrounding the burn and then flushing the areas with saline may be tolerated by the dog. An Elizabethan collar may be used to prevent the Stafford licking the area. In cases showing signs of serious shock, intravenous fluid therapy may be a necessity.

CALCULI (BLADDER STONES)
Stones were often thought to be the cause of straining to pass urine, and where these signs are shown a veterinary examination for bladder inflammation (cystitis) or tumours is advised. Calculi are deposits of mineral salts from the urine, either in the neck of the bladder or nearer the base of the

penis in the male. Stones can also form in the kidneys and these cause pain as they enter the ureters; the bladder is not affected at first.

Calculi are recognisable on X-ray or with ultrasound examinations. The obstruction may be partial when the dog or bitch spends an unusually long time passing urine, or, more frequently in males, no urine can be voided. The dog will strain, looking uncomfortable or in pain. An operation is usually necessary to remove calculi, and dietary advice will be given on how to avoid further attacks. Increasing the dog's water intake and providing opportunities for frequent bladder emptying are equally important in prevention.

CANCER – CARCINOMA
The frequency of cancer in Staffordshire Bull Terriers is no greater than any other breed, but as dogs are now living longer, owners are more likely to be faced with a cancerous diagnosis, particularly in the dog's later years. One in every four dogs will be likely to have one of the many types of cancer.

CATARACTS
Any opaqueness of the lens of the eye is termed a cataract. The dog may become blind, with the condition giving the eye a pearl-like quality. Cataracts most commonly appear in old age or in dogs with diabetes. However, they can occur in young dogs, following an injury such as a thorn piercing the eye. Once the

The responsible owner should learn the basics of first-aid.

condition has been diagnosed, cataract surgery performed at specialised ophthalmic centres can be very successful. See also Hereditary Cataract under Inherited Disorders (page 142).

CONSTIPATION
Unless the Stafford is known to have consumed large quantities of bone or fibrous matter, straining may well be due to an enlarged prostate gland in the male, or any foreign body in the rectum. Increasing the fluid intake and the medication with liquid paraffin is advised, but if the problem persists, the vet should be consulted.

CYSTITIS
Inflammation of the bladder is more common in the bitch, and

may first be noticed when the animal strains frequently, passing only small quantities of urine. Bladder calculi are fairly common in both sexes and will cause cystitis, but bacteria reaching the bladder from outside the body is the usual cause. In all cases the fluid intake should be reviewed since a good 'wash through' of the bladder will reduce the risk of bacteria and mineral particles irritating the bladder lining. Medication with antispasmodics and an appropriate antibiotic will be required.

DIABETES
Dogs suffer from two types of diabetes, but the more common is 'sugar diabetes' known as DM (diabetes mellitus), and is seen more frequently in the older

bitch. It is caused by a lack of insulin to regulate the level of glucose in the blood. The signs of increased thirst, passing large quantities of urine, eye cataracts and muscle weakness are associated with increased appetite and weight loss as the dog attempts to satisfy the variations of its sugar levels. Diagnosis by urine and blood samples is followed by the injection of suitable insulin subcutaneously once or more daily. Some types of endocrine disease, such as diabetes, may arise as a result of an immune-mediated destruction of glandular tissues.

Diabetes insipidus is uncommon in dogs and is related to the water control mechanism of the kidneys.

Vaccination has dramatically reduced the incidence of infectious diseases such as distemper.

GASTRO-ENTERITIS

Vomiting is relatively common in dogs, and it can be a protective mechanism to prevent poisonous substances entering the body. Gastro-enteritis includes diarrhoea attacks, which is a similar process, getting rid of undesirable intestine contents by washing them out. The production of extra mucus and intestinal fluid is seen with a rapid bowel evacuation movement. Both products of gastro-enteritis are objectionable: distressing to the dog and unpleasant for the owner, who may have to clean up afterwards. There are many causes, ranging from the simplest of the dog needing worming, to the complex interaction of viruses and bacteria that can cause an infection to spread through a kennel of dogs.

Dietary diarrhoea may occur after any sudden change in diet, scavenging (as when a packet of butter is stolen), or allergy to a particular food substance or an additive. Where the signs of gastro-enteritis last more than 48 hours, a vet should be prepared to take samples and other tests to look for diseases, such as pancreatitis, colitis or tumours, among many other possible causes, since some disorders may be life-threatening.

Treatment at home may be tried using the principle of 'bowel rest', stopping feeding for 48-72 hours, and allowing fluids in repeated, small quantities. Ice cubes in place of water in the bowl may help reduce vomiting.

DISTEMPER

Fortunately, distemper is now a rare virus infection but at one time it caused devastating illnesses. Routine vaccination has been very effective in preventing disease but there is always the threat of a Stafford acquiring the infection if there has been a breakdown in the immune system. Affected dogs develop a high temperature, cough, diarrhoea and a purulent eye discharge. After several weeks, illness complications may still set in with pneumonia or damage to the nervous system shown as nerve twitchings, paralysis or fits.

EPILEPSY AND FITS

Seizures occur relatively commonly in dogs and represent an acute, and usually brief, disturbance of normal electrical activity in the brain. However, it can be distressing for both the patient and the owner. Most fits last only a short time (under two minutes) and owners often telephone for veterinary advice once the seizure is over. Fits can sometimes occur close together.

Following a fit, the dog should be examined by a veterinary surgeon as soon as possible, even if the seizure has stopped. Some fits are prolonged or very frequent; such seizures may cause permanent brain damage. Once the fits have passed, the dog may seem dull or confused for several hours. Medication is used to control fits, but long-term treatment may be needed.

Electrolyte solutions will help with rehydration. Once signs are alleviated, small feeds of smooth foods (such as steamed fish or chicken) with boiled rice may be gradually introduced. Where there is continual diarrhoea for three to four weeks, the disease is unlikely to resolve without identifying a specific cause and using appropriate treatment.

HEARTWORM DISEASE

Heartworms are becoming more common in the UK but are a major problem in the USA, where they are spread by mosquitoes. Dogs may be protected from six to eight weeks of age with a monthly dose of the medication advised by the veterinarian. There are a number of products available. A blood test can be used to see if the heartworm antigen is present before commencing treatment and it can be repeated annually. The filarial worms live in the heart and blood vessels of the lungs and cause signs such as tiring, intolerance of exercise and a soft deep cough. Heart failure leads to decline and an early death.

There are many other disorders of heart valves and blood vessels that cause a weakening of the heart muscle

FRACTURES

Most broken bones are the result of injury. An old dog with kidney disease may have brittle bones but spontaneous fractures are quite rare. Treatment of fractures will require the attention of the vet; there is little point in attempting first-aid, as the Stafford will be in pain and will adopt the most comfortable position he can find. Natural painkillers, known as endorphins, come into action immediately following such an injury.

If there is a skin wound associated with the fracture, it should be covered to reduce bacterial contamination, thus reducing the risk of osteomyelitis before the break in the bone can be satisfactorily repaired. X-rays will be necessary to confirm a crack or a major displacement of bones.

known as myocardial degeneration. A veterinary cardiologist may be consulted for many heart disorders before a suitable treatment is found.

HEPATITIS

Inflammation of the liver may be due to a virus, but it is uncommon in dogs that have been protected with vaccines that also prevent the bacteria leptospira damaging the liver. Chronic liver disease may be due to heart failure, tumours or some type of toxicity: dietary treatment may help if there are no specific medicines to use.

HIP DYSPLASIA

See Inherited Disorders (page 142).

INVERTEBRAL DISC DISEASE AND PARALYSIS

Collapse or sudden weakness of the hindquarters may be due to pressure on the nerves of the spine that supply the muscles and other sensory receptors. The 'slipped disc', as it is commonly known, may be responsible but any injury to the spine, a fibro cartilage embolism, a fracture or a tumour may cause similar paralysis. The signs are similar, with dragging one or both hind legs, lack of tail use, and often the loss of bladder and bowel control. X-rays, a neurological assessment and possibly an MRI scan will be needed to be certain of the cause. Some cases respond well to surgical correction but others will receive medical treatment, which may be effective and is less costly. Home nursing care should keep the dog clean and groomed, help with bladder or bowel movement, and carry out any physiotherapy advised by the veterinary surgeon. Sudden movements, in the case of spinal fractures, must be avoided.

LEPTOSPIROSIS

Dogs that live in the country or swim in water may be more prone to this infection. Leptospira bacteria carried by rats may be found in pools and

It is rare for a dog to be affected by heartworm in the UK, but it is a common occurrence in the USA.

raise suspicions if similar signs develop, especially if a rash appears around the bite and spreads quickly. Treatment is effective; blood tests can be used to confirm the disease at the laboratory.

MANGE MITES
Several types of mange mites affect dogs and may be the cause of scratching, hair loss and ear disease. Demodectic mange is a skin problem associated with close-coated breeds and is diagnosed by skin scrapes or from plucked hairs. It is probably transmitted from the bitch to the puppy when it first suckles, but may not show as skin disease for several months. Specific treatment is available from the vet, who should be consulted about any unusual skin rash or swellings.

Several other mange types affecting dogs are recognised and may be the cause of scratching, hair loss and ear disease. Sarcoptic mange causes the most irritation and is diagnosed by skin scraping and blood tests. Otodectic mange occurs in the ears and the mite can be found in the wax. Cheyletiella is a surface mite of the coat; it causes white 'dandruff' signs and is diagnosed by coat brushing or Sellotape impressions for microscope inspection. These mite infections first need identifying, but can then be treated with acaracide medication, such as amitraz, selamectin or imidacloprid and moxidectin, provided by the vet.

ditches where rodents may have visited. Annual vaccination against the two types of leptospira is advised. Treatment in the early stages using antibiotics is effective, but liver and kidney damage may permanently incapacitate the Stafford if the early signs, with a fever, are not recognised. Kidney and liver failure will lead to death. Treatment with antibiotics for two to three weeks is needed to prevent the dog carrying leptospira and infecting others.

LYME DISEASE BORRELIOSIS
The tick-borne disease affecting dogs, humans, and, to a lesser extent, other domestic animals is common in the USA; it is estimated that there may be a thousand cases a year in the UK. Often, it is seen as a sudden lameness with a fever or, in the chronic form, one or two joints are affected with arthritis. Often lameness in the carpus (wrist joint) alerts the Stafford owner to this disease. Exposure to ticks (Ixodes ricinus in Britain) should

Repeat treatments after 10 to 14 days are needed to prevent reinfestation.

NEPHRITIS

Dogs may suffer acute kidney failure after poisoning, obstructions to the bladder, or after shock with reduced blood supply. Chronic nephritis is more common in older dogs where the blood accumulates waste products that the damaged kidneys cannot remove. The nephritic syndrome is caused by an immune-mediated damage within the kidney. The signs of increased thirst, loss of appetite and progressive weight loss are commonly seen with kidney disease.

Treatment of chronic renal failure is not reversible but it aims to reduce the load on the remaining filter units (nephrons) and prevent further damage. Fluid intake should be encouraged; if the dog is vomiting, intravenous drips will be needed to provide the liquid to help the kidney to work. Taking the dog outside frequently to help bladder emptying is helpful, too. The vet may advise a special diet, and will probably take repeated blood samples to monitor the kidneys' workload. If the ill Staffordshire Terrier does not eat,

KENNEL COUGH

The signs of a goose-honking cough, hacking or retching that lasts for days to several weeks is due to damage at the base of the windpipe and bronchial tubes. The dry and unproductive cough is caused by a combination of viruses, bacteria and mycoplasma. Vaccination is helpful in preventing the diseases but may not give full protection, as strains of kennel cough seem to vary. The disease is highly contagious and spread by droplets, so it may be acquired at dog shows or boarding kennels. An incubation period of five to seven days is usual. Veterinary treatments alleviate the cough and reduce the duration of the illness.

he will start drawing on his own body protein, and the condition known as azotaemia will result with severe consequences.

A diet of high biological value protein low in phosphate but rich in vitamin B will be advised. Diuretics to produce more urine may be used in the nephritic syndrome cases.

OTITIS EXTERNA

Ear diseases are more common in dogs that have hanging down ear flaps, so Staffords are less affected with ear problems than many others. When otitis occurs, a strong-smelling discharge develops and the dog shakes his head or may show a head tilt. Repeated scratching and head shaking may cause a blood haematoma, as a swelling underneath the skin of the ear flap.

The presence of a grass seed in the ear canal should always be suspected in dogs that have been out in long grass in the summer months. After becoming trapped by the hair, the seed can quickly work its way down the ear canal and can even penetrate the ear drum. The spikes of the grass seed prevent it being shaken out of the ear and veterinary extraction of the seed is essential.

PARVOVIRUS

The virus that infects younger dogs is most dangerous to the recently weaned puppy. Vaccination schedules are devised to protect susceptible dogs, and the vet should be asked as to when and how often a parvo vaccine should be used in a particular locality. The virus has an incubation of about three to five days and attacks the bowels with a sudden onset of vomiting and diarrhoea. Blood may be passed, dehydration sets in and sudden death is possible.

Isolation from other puppies is essential; the replacement of the fluids and electrolytes lost is urgent. Medication to stop the vomiting, antibiotics against secondary bacteria and, later, a smooth, bland diet may be provided.

Staffordshire Bull Terriers living in the country are more likely to be affected by Lyme disease.

PROSTATE DISEASE

Elderly Stafford males that have not been castrated may show signs of straining, which may be thought to be a sign of constipation, but an enlarged prostate gland at the neck of the bladder will often be the real cause. Most often it is a benign enlargement that causes pressure into the rectum, rather than it blocking the bladder exit. Once diagnosed, hormone injections combined with a laxative diet may be very effective.

PYODERMA

A term used by some vets for a bacterial skin infection, it is a condition often seen in demodectic mange infections, but it is also associated with a wet, oozing skin known as 'wet eczema'. Treatment should be given to prevent licking and

scratching, clipping away hair to encourage a dry surface where bacteria cannot multiply so readily; an appropriate antibiotic can be used. If the bacteria tunnels inwards, it results in the furunculosis skin disorder, which is more difficult to treat.

PYOMETRA

At one time, pyometra was the commonest cause of illness in middle-aged to elderly bitches. This disease of the uterus would be seen in bitches never bred from and those who had had litters earlier in life. The cause is a hormone imbalance that prepares the lining of the uterus for puppies, but fluid and mucus accumulates, leading to an acute illness if bacteria invade the organ. Known as 'open pyometra' when a blood-stained mucoid discharge comes out, often sticking to the

hairs around the vulva, it has been confused with a bitch coming on heat unexpectedly.

It can be more difficult to diagnose the cause of illness when there is no discharge present, known as 'closed pyometra', and other ways of testing the patient for the uterus disorder may be employed by the vet. Although medical treatments are available, it is more usual to perform a hysterectomy, especially if the bitch has come to the end of her breeding career.

RABIES

The fatal virus infection is almost unknown in the UK, but it remains as a cause of death of animals and some humans in parts of the world where the preventive vaccine is not in regular use. The disease attacks a dog's central nervous system; it is spread by infective saliva usually following a bite from an animal that is developing the disease. An annual rabies vaccination is an important way of controlling the disease.

RINGWORM

This is a fungal disease of the skin that has nothing to do with worms, but it acquired the name from the circular red marks on the skin following infection. It may appear as bald, scaly patches and will spread to children or adults handling the dog unless precautions are taken. Treatments will vary depending on the extent of the problem.

VESTIBULAR DISEASE

Older Staffords may be subject to a condition of a head tilt, often with eye-flicking movements (known as nystagmus). At one time it was commonly diagnosed as a stroke because of its sudden onset. The dog may circle or fall on one side, and then roll, unable to balance himself.

Vestibular disease develops suddenly but, unlike the equivalent human stroke, there is no sign of bleeding or of a vascular accident in the brain. Recovery may take place slowly as the balance centre of the brain regains its use after one to three weeks. Treatment by the vet will assist a return to normal, although some dogs always carry their head with a tilt.

INHERITED DISORDERS

Genetic defects and disorders have been with us a long time but improved veterinary diagnostic methods and the fact that now that dogs live longer make it more likely that degenerative diseases are able to show themselves, perhaps undue emphasis has been placed on some inherited disorders. Healthy parents to breed puppies, should always be selected.

CLEFT PALATE

It is not a major breed problem but the abnormality is seen from time to time in new born puppies; they have obvious difficulty in feeding when sucking the mother's milk. The condition allows food or fluid to enter the nasal respiratory passage and is often associated with the more obvious 'hare lip' where the two sides of the upper lips have failed to join whilst the embryo was developing in the uterus.

HEREDITARY CATARACT

A test for the gene mutation that causes a form of blindness soon after birth is now available for

The Stafford has rose or half-pricked ears, and is less likely to be affected by ear diseases than breeds with drop ears.

Pyometra is a life-threatening condition in bitches.

this cause of blindness. A 3ml blood sample or a cheek swab can be taken and sent off to a designated laboratory (The Animal Health Trust in the UK provide such a service). Results when obtained from the lab will come as 'Clear', 'Carrier' or 'Affected'. Consultation with a veterinary surgeon will decide on a course of action if either of the second two categories is reported

POLAR CATARACTS

Cataracts are a loss of transparency in the lens of the eye and this can be expected in many elderly dogs. Ageing changes can also cause blueness in the eye from 'lenticular sclerosis' which can be differentiated from cataracts by the veterinarian using an ophthalmoscope and slit lamp. Cataracts are classified on the part of the lens first affected, posterior cortical cataracts occur for various reasons including hereditary and secondary to retinal degeneration. Polar cataracts may occur in the centre of the lens and have an inherited cause. Posterior polar cataracts may be present as a small dot on the inside of the lens but cause little trouble and do not progress to blindness.

PHPV

When the foetus is developing in the bitch, the developing eye lens is fed by a small artery from the retina, in some dogs traces of this may be found by the veterinary ophthalmologist. PHPV (persistent hyperplastic primary vitreous) occurs when these fetal vessels supplying the lens are

Staffords. The condition of cataract or opaqueness of the lens in the dog's eye had been identified over 30 years ago, the mutation has been passed down though subsequent generations of Staffords and it has a recessive form of inheritance. Carriers of the condition may show no abnormality in their eyes but when mated with another carrier a litter of affected pups may result, but perhaps only a quarter of those born become blind later. The eyes seem normal when the lids open 10-12 days after birth, but the cataracts may then appear weeks or several months later and will then progress to total blindness over the next few years. Litters of puppies can be examined from 8 weeks and older for this inherited disorder.

Identifying this condition in potential parents for breeding is an important step in eliminating hyperplastic (overlarge) and do not undergo normal regression. Small changes can be seen by the vet as pigmented dots on the posterior lens capsule but without concurrent cataract. The more severe changes that may lead to secondary cataract and blindness occur only rarely in the Staffordshire bull terrier. Puppies can be tested from 6 weeks by a veterinary ophthalmologist as a schedule A congenital inherited ocular disease. The mode of inheritance is complex but is thought to be an irregular dominant gene with a variable expression. The Staffordshire Bull Terrier also suffers less from posterior lens capsule deformities but in this PHPV disorder it may develop folds or rosettes in the retina at the back of the eye as well.

It is imperative to select healthy breeding stock to limit the possibility of inherited disease.

HIP DYSPLASIA

An inherited disease in many breeds of dog, it does affect some Staffords but the breed average score is at a lower level than many working breeds. Hip dysplasia disease is a malformation of both the femoral head and acetabulum 'cup' of the hip, which results in lameness, pain and eventual arthritic changes. X-rays can be taken to measure the joint and a score is awarded by a specialist who reads the photo plates. It is not a major problem in the breed but anyone buying a puppy should enquire about the hip state of the parents before completing the purchase.

Surgical treatments can be used to correct a hip abnormality, but most can be controlled through regular exercise, muscle building and the use of anti-inflammatory medication.

NEUROLOGICAL DISEASE DUE TO L-2-HYDROXYGLUTARIC ACIDURIA

As a result of studies in America and the UK on the structure of the canine genome, it has been possible to pinpoint a number of hereditary disorders by testing for a specific DNA defect. The ability to recognise the cause of unusual behaviour, ataxia (unsteady walking) and seizures (fits) became possible in 2001 in affected Staffordshire Bull Terriers and subsequently in another breed (West Highland White Terrier). Affected dogs can show a variety of symptoms including dementia, seizures, tremors and ataxia. In the past it was sometimes mis-diagnosed as epilepsy from the symptoms shown and the dog's abnormal behaviour. An accumulation of L-2 Hydroxyglutaric Acid in the body fluids of the dog could be shown in urine tests, and now scanning tests on the brain with M R I imaging are positive in identifying this disease. Previously there was no way of identifying this neuro-metabolic condition by clinical signs and there is still no known treatment for the disease. The DNA (or gene) test is now available from specialist laboratories such as the Animal Health Trust in the UK, Optigen, Health Gene and PennGen in the USA. It can identify carrier dogs that are then considered unsuitable for breeding with other carrier or untested dogs and can also be used to identify dogs that already have the disease.

OSTEOCHONDROSIS OF THE ELBOW

Surgery is needed if lameness developing from a cartilage abnormality causes a permanent limp. It must first be diagnosed by taking several X rays of the affected elbow; the stifle joint my also develop this condition and the vet's advice should be sought.

PATELLAR LUXATION

The slipping out of place of the kneecap is often an inherited disease in smaller breeds but it may be the result of a torn ligament after jumping. Staffords that may be affected seem to move normally then start limping on a back leg – sometimes so much that the affected leg is held up. The hock is rotated outwards as the patellar is out of its normal groove and slips inwardly (medial). The condition is not painful and gentle bending up of the leg may unlock the patellar so it slips back into the correct place. Surgery is quite successful in curing the condition.

PORTO–SYSTEMIC LIVER SHUNT

Abnormal blood vessels that run through the liver prevent the organ functioning properly and death may occur at a relatively young age after a prolonged illness. It is a rare disease but some affected puppies do not thrive and die young. Others may have less severe illness and only when tests on the liver are made is the disease recognised.

Umbilical hernia operations on

Increasingly owners are becoming more aware of the effectiveness of complementary therapies.

young puppies to correct a bulge in the 'belly button' are sometimes required. It is a fairly minor procedure but the condition should be watched for when purchasing a puppy.

COMPLEMENTARY THERAPIES

There are many treatments that can be given to dogs over and above the type of medical or surgical treatment that you might have expected by attending a veterinary surgery. Some of these alternative treatments have proved to benefit dogs, whilst others are better known for their use in humans where the placebo effect of an additional therapy has a

strong influence on the benefit received.

PHYSIOTHERAPY

This is one of the longest tested treatments used in injuries and after surgery on the limbs. Chartered physiotherapists and veterinary nurses who have studied the subject work under the direction of the vet who is ready to advise or apply procedures that will help mobility and recovery. Massage, heat, exercise or electrical stimulation are used to relieve pain, regain movement and restore muscle strength.

HYDROTHERAPY

This is a popular therapy, as Staffords enjoy the use of water for the treatment of joint disease, injuries, or for the maintenance of fitness and health.

ACUPUNCTURE

This therapy has a long history of healing derived from Chinese medicine, involving the insertion of fine needles into specific locations in the body known as 'acupuncture points'. The placing of the needles to stimulate nervous tissue is based on human charts, and very good results have been reported when veterinary acupuncturists have been allowed to select suitable cases to treat.

REIKI

This involves the laying on of the

therapist's hands, and can have beneficial results. The advantage is that it does not involve the dog tolerating needles in his body, but, to date, there are few qualified veterinary operators.

MAGNETIC THERAPY

This therapy is perhaps more questionable in observed results. It involves magnetic products that are applied to the dog to relieve pain and increase mobility.

AROMATHERAPY

This involves treating dogs with remedies that would have once been found in the wild. It involves the use of selected essential oils and plant extracts.

PHYTOTHERAPY OR HERBAL MEDICINE

This has proven benefits, and there are an ever-increasing number of veterinary surgeons skilled in selecting appropriate plant products. Natural remedies are attractive to many users and provide a good alternative to many conventional veterinary treatments.

Herbal drugs have become increasingly popular and their use is widespread, but licensing regulations and studies on interactions between herbal

With good care and management, your Stafford should live a long, happy and healthy life.

products and other veterinary medicines are still incomplete. Often a complex mixture of herbs will be prescribed, and it is not always clear which ones are effective. For example, a prescription for skin disease might include Calendula officinalis (marigold flower) for its antimicrobial, antifungal effects, Echinacea spp. (coneflower root) as an antimicrobial and immune stimulant, Rehmannia glutinosa (rehmannia root) as an anti-inflammatory, antiallergic and 'blood tonic', Valeriana officinalis (valerian root) as a nerve sedative, Taraxacum officinale (dandelion root) as a liver stimulant and laxative, Urtica dioica (nettle leaf) for its antihistamine effect and Glycyrrhiza glabra (liquorice root) as another anti-inflammatory.

As with all alternative therapies, you need to consult a person who has the experience and specialist knowledge of applying the treatments. The Stafford's own vet should be informed, since some veterinary medicines should not be used when other remedies are involved.

THE CONTRIBUTORS

THE EDITOR: ALEC WATERS (ASHSTOCK)

Alec was involved with breeding and showing Staffordshire Bull Terriers for over 35 years, and his Ashstock affix is known worldwide.

He bred 7 UK Champions that include Ch Ashstock Artful Bess, Ch Ashstock Max The Miller, Ch Ashstock Brinchester, Ch Ashstock Lucky Jim, Ch Ashstock Red Buttons, Ch Ashstock Black Maria, Ch Ashstock By Jupiter JW.

Alec bred Ashstock Wild Colonial Boy who gained 2CCs but was tragically killed at an early age by a road accident and Ashstock Scarlett Buttons who gained 1CC & 1RCC.

In addition Alec bred 7 overseas champions that include Aust Ch Ashstock Mad Hatter (sire of the year for 3 years running), Aust Ch Colonial Force of Ashstock Multi BIS and sire of Multi BIS winners, Aust Ch Ashstock Old Hat and many other major winners.

He was a UK and international Championship show judge and he judged extensively throughout Europe as well as Australia, America, Israel, South Africa and New Zealand.

He had the honour of judging Staffordshire Bull Terriers at Crufts in 1980.

Alec was a Member of the Kennel Club and was Chairman of the Staffordshire Bull Terrier Breed Council for Great Britain & Northern Ireland for 7 years. He served on many breed club committees and was life vice president of the Southern Counties Staffordshire Bull Terrier Society and the East Anglian Staffordshire Bull Terrier Club, and he was elected Kennel Club Breed Liason Officer.

Alec was Patron for 15 years of the Staffordshire Bull Terrier Society of NSW, Australia's Foundation Club since 1965 and an Honorary Member of Gesellschaft der Bullterrier-Freunde in Germany.

In addition Alec had considerable experience of appearing in the courts as an expert witness in defence of the Staffordshire Bull Terrier.
See Chapter Seven: The Perfect Staffordshire Bull Terrier.

JENNY SMITH (WILLOWSTAFF)

Jenny first became active in the breed in 1985 when, along with husband Mick, they purchased their first two Staffordshire Bull Terriers – thus began a hobby and love of the breed, which, to date, has spanned over 20 years. The Willowstaff kennel name was first registered in 1989 and more recently Sally Cox has joined the partnership. Several dogs have been campaigned under the Willowstaff affix, most notably Willowstaff Guardian Spirit RCC, litter sister Willowstaff Dark Crystal RCC, Willowstaff Poetry N Motion JW and Steelyard Innovator at Willowstaff JW. They are currently campaigning Willowstaff Barbed Wire, Willowstaff Evolution and Willowstaff Poetic Justice.

A Championship show judge of Staffordshire Bull Terriers, Jenny has completed appointments at the Potteries SBT Club (Bitches, 2005) and Midland Counties Canine Society (both sexes, 2006). In addition, Jenny and Mick had the great honour of judging the SBT Club of Northern New South Wales

(Australia) Inaugural Championship Show weekend in September 2005.

Jenny held the position of Public Relations Officer to the SBT Breed Council of Great Britain & Northern Ireland from 1998-2002. In addition, she has had a long association with the Notts & Derby District SBT Club, culminating in her appointment as Club Secretary in 2002; a position she holds to date.
See Chapter One: Getting To Know The Staffordshire Bull Terrier, and material on New Challenges in Chapter Six: Training And Socialisation.

JIM BEAUFOY (WYREFARE)

Jim was introduced to his first Stafford in 1961, and he has dedicated himself exclusively to the breed ever since. As an international Championship show judge in Staffords, he has had the privilege to judge the breed on numerous occasions at the highest level in Germany, Sweden, Eire, Italy, Spain, Holland, Austria, the United States, South Africa, Australia, and New Zealand. Having also judged the breed at Championship level on many occasions in the UK, he is proud to have achieved the once-in-a-lifetime honour of judging Staffords at Crufts in 2006.

Jim has been involved with the parent club of the breed, The Staffordshire Bull Terrier Club, and has served as secretary for very many years, still retaining that position today. He is a past Chairman of the Staffordshire Bull Terrier Breed Council for Great Britain and Northern Ireland, and has considerable experience of appearing in the courts as an expert witness in defence of the Staffordshire Bull Terrier.

Together with his wife and daughter, both themselves international Championship show judges in the breed, Jim is a regular exhibitor with the family Wyrefare Staffords, the most widely known of which is Ch. And Ir. Champion Wyrefare Prince Naseem, sire of numerous Champions of the breed worldwide.
See Chapter Two: The First Staffordshire Bull Terriers.

CLARE LEE (CONSTONES)

Clare grew up with Staffords – as a young girl showing some of the dogs belonging to her father, Nap Cairns. In the 1960s she and her husband, Tony, joined with her father in the Constones prefix. All the Constones dogs trace back to the first bitch bought by Nap Cairns in 1942. This is now the oldest, active prefix in the breed. Prior to the 1960s there had been three all-male Champions from this kennel. Since the 1960s, the partnership added three more: Ch. Constones Compact, Ch. Constones Grim Girl and Ch. Constones Yer Man (at one time the breed record holder), Top Dog in the breed in 1989 and 1990, and Top Sire in 1990. The sire of 11 Champions, he retired from the show-ring after winning Best of Breed at the Centenary Crufts in 1991. Since the death of Nap, Clare and Tony have added two more Champions to the tally: Ch. Constones High Five and Ch. Constones Jump for Joy. In addition to Champions, there have been many other winners from this kennel at home and

abroad – including Australian Ch. Constones Hells Bells.

Clare has been judging at Championship level for nearly 40 years, including at Crufts 1985 – the fiftieth anniversary year of the breed's recognition. She has judged throughout Europe, as well as in Russia, Australia, Canada, the US and South Africa.

For a number of years Clare was Secretary of the Northern Counties SBT Club, of which she has been made a Life Vice President. She has written/edited two books on the Breed and is the present breed correspondent for the *Dog World* weekly journal.
See Chapter Three; A Stafford for your Lifestyle, and Chapter Five: The Best of Care.

NORMA VANN (VANORIC)

Norma had her first Staffordshire Bull Terrier in the early 1980s in partnership with her husband, Richard. They became members of the East Midlands SBT Club in 1984 and an interest in showing Staffords quickly grew into a passion. Norma got involved in Stafford rescue and has worked tirelessly as rescue co-ordinator for the Midlands area. She has served on the committee of the East Midlands SBT Club since 1991, and was elected secretary in 1995 – a position she still holds today.

Norma and Richard have campaigned a number of Staffords under their Vanoric affix. Success came with Might Tiger, The Storm Maiden of Vanoric, Ch. Jamavins Femme Fatale of Vanoric and homebred Ch. Vanoric Voo Doo who was to become the top Stafford of all time with 26 Challenge Certificates, 17 Reserve CCS. Groups 1,2,3 and 4. Voo Doo's success was to make Norma and Richard top breeders for two years running.

Norma first judged Staffordshire Bull Terriers in 1990 and now judges at Championship show level. She has been fortunate to judge in most parts of the UK as well as overseas.
See Chapter Four: The New Arrival.

JULIA BARNES

Julia has owned and trained a number of different dog breeds, and is a puppy socialiser for Dogs for the Disabled, and is a former journalist. She has written many books, including several on dog training and behaviour. Julia is indebted to Jenny Smith for her material on New Challenges and her specialist knowledge of Staffordshire Bull Terriers.
See Chapter Six: Training and Socialisation

DICK LANE BScFRAgSFRCVS

Dick qualified from the Royal Veterinary College and spent most of his time in veterinary practice in Warwickshire. He had a particular interest in assistance dogs: working for the Guide Dogs for the Blind Association and more recently for Dogs for the Disabled as a founder Trustee. Dick has been awarded a Fellowship of the Royal College of Veterinary Surgeons and a Fellowship of the Royal Agricultural Societies. He has recently completed an Honours BSc in Applied Animal Behaviour and Training, awarded by the University of Hull.
See Chapter Eight: Happy and Healthy.

USEFUL ADDRESSES

BREED CLUBS

Alyn and Deeside Staffordshire Bull Terrier Club
Secretary: Mrs Paula Williams
Telephone: 01244 671405

Downlands Staffordshire Bull Terrier Club
Secretary: Mrs A Gatenby
Telephone: 01730 828402
Website: http://www.downlands.org.uk/

East Anglian Staffordshire Bull Terrier Club
Secretary: Mrs L McFadyen
Telephone: 01205 871762
Web: http://www.eastangliansbtclub.co.uk/

East Midlands Staffordshire Bull Terrier Club
Secretary: Mrs N Vann
Telephone: 01664 840570
Web: http://www.emsbtc.co.uk/

Merseyside Staffordshire Bull Terrier Club
Secretary: Mrs C Kerrigan
Telephone: 01515 467516
Web: http://www.msbtc.co.uk/

Morecambe Bay and Cumbria Staffordshire Bull Terrier Club
Secretary: Mrs Sheila Dootson
Telephone: 01617 895584

North Eastern Staffordshire Bull Terrier Club
Acting Secretary: Mr G Jackson
Telephone: 01915 214682

North of Scotland Staffordshire Bull Terrier Club
Secretary: Miss J A Smith
Telephone: 01569 760418

North West Staffordshire Bull Terrier Club
Secretary: Miss S Houghton
Telephone: 01942 708161

Northern Counties Staffordshire Bull Terrier Club
Secretary: Mrs L King
Telephone: 0113 2632 462
Web: www.ncsbtc.org.uk

Northern Ireland Staffordshire Bull Terrier Club
Secretary: Mr C Erwin
Telephone: 028 9081 3704

Notts and Derby District Staffordshire Bull Terrier Club
Secretary: Mrs Jenny Smith
Telephone: 01332 781062
Web: http://www.NDDSBTC.co.uk

Potteries Staffordshire Bull Terrier Club
Secretary: Mrs S A Reader
Telephone: 01782 611514
Web: http://www.psbtc.org.uk/

Scottish Staffordshire Bull Terrier Club
Secretary: Mr Fleming
Telephone: 0141 763 2349

Southern Counties Staffordshire Bull Terrier Society
Secretary: Mr J Joyce
Telephone: 020 8310 9669

Staffordshire Bull Terrier Breed Council of Great Britain and Northern Ireland
Secretary: Miss Jaci McLauchlan
Telephone: 01642 783948
Web: http://www.staffords.co.uk

Staffordshire Bull Terrier Club
Secretary: Mr J Beaufoy
Telephone: 01299 403382
Web: http://www.thesbtc.com/

Staffordshire Bull Terrier Club of South Wales
Secretary: Mr K Jones
Telephone: 01639 821410
Web: http://www.sbtcsw.co.uk/

Western Staffordshire Bull Terrier Society
Secretary: Leanne Ferguson
Telephone: 07974 483679
Email: leanne@leanne11.fsnet.co.uk
Web: http://www.wsbts.co.uk

KENNEL CLUBS

American Kennel Club (AKC)
5580 Centerview Drive
Raleigh, NC 27606
Telephone: 919 233 9767
Fax: 919 233 3627
Email: info@akc.org
Web: www.akc.org

The Kennel Club (UK)
1 Clarges Street
London, W1J 8AB
Telephone: 0870 606 6750
Fax: 0207 518 1058
Web: www.thekennelclub.org.uk

TRAINING AND BEHAVIOUR

Association of Pet Dog Trainers (APDT)
PO Box 17, Kempsford, GL7 4W7
Telephone: 01285 810811
Email: APDToffice@aol.com
Web: http://www.apdt.co.uk

Association of Pet Behaviour Counsellors (APBC)
PO BOX 46, Worcester, WR8 9YS
Telephone: 01386 751151
Fax: 01386 750743
Email: info@apbc.org.uk
Web: http://www.apbc.org.uk/

ACTIVITIES

Agility Club
http://www.agilityclub.co.uk/

British Flyball Association
PO Box 109, Petersfield, GU32 1XZ
Telephone: 01753 620110
Fax: 01726 861079
Email: bfa@flyball.org.uk
Web: http://www.flyball.org.uk/

World Canine Freestyle Organisation
P.O. Box 350122, Brooklyn, NY 11235-2525, USA
Telephone: 718 332-8336
Fax: 718 646-2686
Email: wcfodogs@aol.com
Web: www.worldcaninefreestyle.org

HEALTH

Alternative Veterinary Medicine Centre
Chinham House, Stanford in the Vale, Oxfordshire, SN7 8NQ
Email: enquiries@bahvs.com
Web: www.bahvs.com

Animal Health Trust
Secretary: Keith Reid
Lanwades Park, Kentford, Newmarket, Suffolk, CB8 7UU
Telephone: 08700 502424
Fax: 08700 502425
Email: info@aht.org.uk
Website: www.aht.org.uk

British Association of Veterinary Ophthalmologists (BAVO)
Email: hjf@vetspecialists.co.uk or secretary@bravo.org.uk
Web: http://www.bravo.org.uk/

British Small Animal Veterinary Association (BSAVA)
Woodrow House, 1 Telford Way, Waterwells Business Park, Quedgeley, Gloucestershire, GL2 2AB
Telephone: 01452 726700
Fax: 01452 726701
Email: customerservices@bsava.com
Web: http://www.bsava.com/

British Veterinary Hospitals Association (BHVA)
Station Bungalow, Main Rd, Stocksfield, Northumberland, NE43 7HJ
Telephone: 07966 901619
Fax: 07813 915954
Email: office@bvha.org.uk
Web: http://www.bvha.org.uk/

Royal College of Veterinary Surgeons (RCVS)
Belgravia House, 62-64 Horseferry Road, London, SW1P 2AF
Telephone: 0207 222 2001
Fax: 0207 222 2004
Email: admin@rcvs.org.uk
Web: www.rcvs.org.uk

ASSISTANCE DOGS

Canine Partners
Mill Lane, Heyshott, Midhurst, West Sussex, GU29 0ED
Telephone: 08456 580480
www.caninepartners.co.uk

Dogs for the Disabled
The Frances Hay Centre, Blacklocks Hill
Banbury, Oxon, OX17 2BS
Telephone: 01295 252600
Web: www.dogsforthedisabled.org

Guide Dogs for the Blind Association
Burghfield Common, Reading, RG7 3YG
Telephone: 01189 835555
Web: www.guidedogs.org.uk/

Hearing Dogs for Deaf People
The Grange, Wycombe Road, Saunderton, Princes Risborough, Bucks, HP27 9NS
Telephone: 01844 348100
Web: hearingdogs.org.uk

Pets as Therapy
3 Grange Farm Cottages, Wycombe Road, Saunderton, Princes Risborough, Bucks, HP27 9NS
Telephone: 0870 977 0003
Web: http://www.petsastherapy.org/

Support Dogs
21 Jessops Riverside, Brightside Lane, Sheffield, S9 2RX
Tel: 0870 609 3476
Web: www.support-dogs.org.uk

Help us turn paws into helping hands

Sponsor a **Dogs for the Disabled** puppy for just £5.00 per month and you could help change someone's life.

www.dogsforthedisabled.org   **Telephone: 01295 252600**

Dogs for the
Disabled
Registered charity number: 1092960